COLORADO

COLORADO BY ROAD

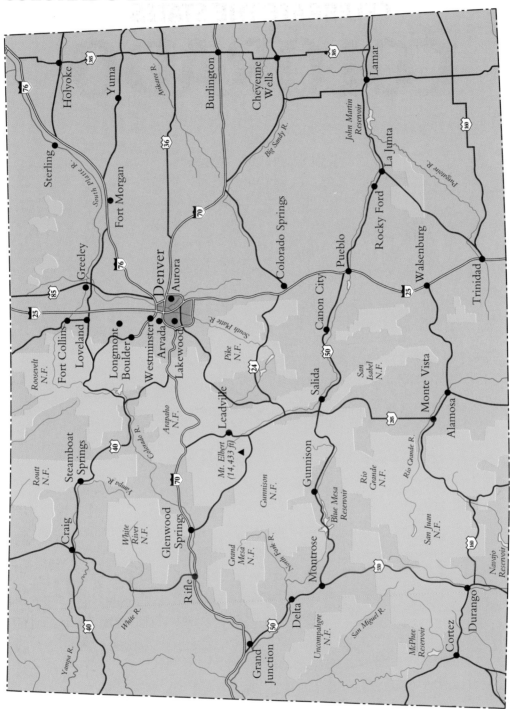

CELEBRATE THE STATES
COLORADO

Eleanor H. Ayer

BENCHMARK BOOKS

MARSHALL CAVENDISH
NEW YORK

Benchmark Books
Marshall Cavendish Corporation
99 White Plains Road
Tarrytown, New York 10591-9001

Library of Congress Cataloging-in-Publication Data
Ayer, Eleanor H.
Colorado / Eleanor H. Ayer
p.   cm. — (Celebrate the states)
Includes bibliographical references and index.
Summary: Surveys the geography, history, people, and customs
of the highest state.
ISBN 0-7614-0148-2 (lib. bdg.)
1. Colorado—Juvenile literature. [1. Colorado.] I. Title. II. Series.
F776.3.A94   1997   978.8—dc20   96-34267   CIP   AC

Maps and graphics supplied by Oxford Cartographers, Oxford, England

Photo research by Ellen Barrett Dudley

Cover photo: *Tom Stack & Associates*, Spencer Swanger

The photographs in this book are used by permission and through the courtesy of: *Tom Stack & Associates:*
Ann Duncan, 6-7, 57, 127; Barbara von Hoffmann, 10-11; Jeff Foott, 21, 124; Terry Donnelly, 48-49;
Tom Stack, 58, 82; Spencer Swanger, 67; Bob Winsett, 67 (inset), 86; Doug Sokell, 114; Rich Buzzelli, 138.
The Image Bank: Michael Melford, 13; Larry J. Pierce, 17; John P. Kelly, 68-69, 76; David W. Hamilton, 78.
Photo Researchers, Inc.: Gary Ladd, 14; Tim Davis, 24; Harvey Stein, 29; G. Guisinger, 61; Jim Steinberg, 71;
Margaret Durrance, 104-105; Carl Purcell, 109; Jeff Lepore, 121 (top); Anthony Mercieca, 121 (bottom);
Spencer Swanger, back cover. *Corbis-Bettmann:* 19, 92, 99, 102, 132 (right), 135 (bottom). *National Museum of
American Art, Washington DC/Art Resource, NY:* 26-27. *Colorado Historical Society:* 31, neg.# F24285, 36;
neg.# F21.977, 37; neg# F40201, 40; neg# F13.030, 41; neg# F21.164, 131. *Museum of Western Art:* 33.
Jack Olson: 39, 44, 47, 55, 62, 74, 76 (inset), 80, 83, 88-89, 107, 129. *BKA/Network Aspen:* 51. *UPI/Corbis-
Bettmann:* 91, 100, 132 (left), 133, 135 (top), 136. *Michael Garman:* 93. *Wendy Shattil/Bob Rozinski:* 95.
Denver Public Library, Western History Department: 97. *Animals Animals:* 112. *Timberline Llamas:* 113.
Glenn Randall: 118.

Printed in Italy

3   5   6   4

CONTENTS

COLORADO IS . . .

Colorado is breathtakingly beautiful.

> O beautiful for spacious skies,
> For amber waves of grain;
> For purple mountain majesties
> Above the fruited plain . . .
> —from *America the Beautiful*, by Katharine Lee Bates,
> inspired by the view from Pikes Peak

"[Colorado's] scenery bankrupts the English language."
—Theodore Roosevelt, twenty-sixth president of the United States

Its beauty has drawn people for centuries . . .

"It was something, at last to stand upon the storm-rent crown of this lonely sentinel of the Rocky Range, on one of the mightiest of the vertebrae of the backbone of the North American continent, and to see the waters start for both oceans."
 —Isabella Bird, Englishwoman who climbed Longs Peak in 1873

"Being Molly for even the six months it took to make the film meant so much to me that I bought a small piece of her Colorado, close to Leadville. . . . I go there as often as possible to enjoy the wonder, beauty and serenity of [the] mountains and give myself a spiritual treat."   —Debbie Reynolds, played Molly Brown in
The Unsinkable Molly Brown

. . . and those who live here tend to stay.

"I will never leave my Shining Mountains . . ."
—Ute Chief Ouray, to United States government agents

"It's great to live in Colorado."
—inscription on the tombstone of Ginny Pankey,
Colorado Representative Phil Pankey's wife

"You move to California because you want heat; you move to Alaska because you want cold, and you move to Mars because you're a non-breathing mutant. But you don't have to move from Colorado because you got it all right here, baby!"
—T. C. Ritz, sixth-grade Colorado student

Besides the state's awesome beauty, the sun shines here three hundred days a year. The outlook of most people is as bright as the Colorado sun. With its golden fields of wheat and corn, its majestic Rocky Mountains, and the opportunity for a year-round outdoor life, it's no wonder newcomers arrive in droves. Some old-timers are saddened by the recent waves of immigrants. They complain about overcrowded highways, huge housing developments, and the "Californication of Colorado." But who can blame people for heeding the words of singer John Denver, "Guess he'd rather be in Colorado . . ."?

1 MILE-HIGH STATE

When western songwriter Utah Phillips sang of "going Out West where the states are square," Colorado was one of the states he had in mind. Actually Colorado (meaning "color red" in Spanish) is more of a rectangle—276 miles north to south and 387 miles east to west.

Some folks say that if you took a giant flatiron to Colorado and pressed down the mountains, you'd have a state as large as Texas. There are fifty-two mountain peaks in Colorado above fourteen thousand feet, and another thousand above ten thousand feet. The state has so many mountains that some of them haven't been named. Colorado is the eighth largest state, and overall it is the highest.

Stretching north to south through the center of the state and into the southwest are Colorado's tallest mountains. They are part of the Rocky Mountains, which run from Canada into Mexico. Colorado has sixteen major ranges. The Front Range, on the eastern side of the Rockies, is the biggest and best known.

Yet the state is by no means *all* mountains. Mountains are one of its three major landforms. In the east are the plains—huge, flat, treeless expanses of grass. In the central and southwest parts of the state are the mountains. Western Colorado is covered by a vast plateau that stretches above the surrounding land.

"Colorado's mountains are certainly its most awesome feature—wild, rugged, and unforgiving." —*Silvia Pettem*, Colorado Mountains and Passes

FRUITED PLAINS AND ROLLING FOOTHILLS

Colorado's High Plains are part of the Great Plains, which spread across the midwestern section of North America. The plains sit on thousands of feet of dirt washed down when the outer edges of the Rocky Mountains eroded. In some places the bed of dirt and rock is almost four miles thick. As the plains slope eastward, farther away from the mountains, the rock bed becomes thinner. Near the Kansas border, the base is only about a mile thick.

The Colorado plains are home to few people and animals, and even fewer trees. When explorer Stephen Harriman Long came west in 1820, he called this area "the Great American desert." The plains, he said, were "almost wholly unfit for cultivation." How wrong he was! Today, thanks to irrigation and improved farming methods, eastern Colorado is one of the largest agricultural regions in the country.

The Front Range runs along the eastern foothills of the Rockies.

Because so many streams rise here, Colorado is known as "The Mother of Rivers."

Eighty percent of Colorado's people live in the strip from Fort Collins south through the Denver/Boulder area to Colorado Springs and Pueblo. Towns sprang up because the settlers who came west along the trails and rivers were stopped here by the mountains. The 2.5 million people who have since settled along this corridor have created an urban sprawl. The Front Range is now largely housing developments with few divisions in between.

The Denver metro area is second only to Los Angeles in poor air quality. Lack of good public transportation means heavy car traffic and high carbon-monoxide levels. The mountains trap this polluted air, creating Denver's ugly "brown cloud." Says fifth grader William Ayer, "They're building too many roads. That's why Denver's getting so polluted." The millions of people who live in this semi-arid climate have created a water shortage. On the upside, this lack of water has become a natural way of limiting growth in Colorado.

THE MOUNTAIN REGION

Colorado's mountains are the source of many of the country's large rivers. Running along the tops of the mountains north to south is an imaginary line called the Continental Divide. Rivers that rise (begin) east of the Divide—including the Platte, Arkansas, Rio Grande, and Big Thompson—flow eventually into the Atlantic Ocean. Rivers that rise on its western side flow into the Pacific. Among these are the Colorado, Gunnison, Green, Yampa, and Dolores.

The San Juan mountains in southwestern Colorado get nearly

eighty inches of precipitation a year, mostly in the form of snow. Each year during spring runoff in the San Juans and elsewhere, rivers fill with water as the snow melts. But sometimes the snow doesn't melt. Year after year it accumulates and eventually turns into ice. When this huge pile of ice is heavy enough to move slowly downhill, a glacier is born.

The state has several glaciers and many large rivers, but few natural lakes. Those that are natural are usually small and found in the high mountains. Most large lakes are reservoirs for water storage, and many of them are manmade.

Even experienced mountaineers can be caught off guard by quick changes in the weather. In the mountains, warns Janet Robertson, author of *Day Hikes on the Colorado Trail*, "Snow storms, gale force winds, stifling heat, [freezing] rains . . . can [happen] on any given summer day." Winter weather can be even more severe.

High altitude plants and animals must be tough to endure harsh weather, to survive in thin air, and to withstand the burning rays of the sun. But they are fragile, too. When hiking boots trample spongy tundra grasses it can take years for the vegetation to recover, if it ever does. Pollution from cities is also very harmful to mountain plant and animal life.

Nestled among the mountain ranges of central Colorado, near the Continental Divide, are four huge natural parks. These large, flat valleys were once covered with soft, green grasses and dotted with herds of buffalo and antelope. Today farmers raise hay and other crops in the parks, and ranchers run large herds of cattle.

The northernmost of these parks is North Park, once a favorite hunting ground of the Ute Indians. Just to the south and west of

"I'd ride four, five days herdin' cattle and never see another soul. It was scary at first, but peaceful."   —*Earl Thomas, cowboy*

the Continental Divide lies Middle Park, where the Colorado River rises. It gets very cold in Middle Park in the winter. The town of Frazer often appears on the news as the "coldest spot in the nation."

In South Park, west of Denver near Fairplay, are the headwaters of the South Platte River. In 1859 prospectors rushed here looking for gold. The fourth and southernmost of the parks, the San Luis

BUFFALO BILL:
THE STORY BEHIND THE LEGEND

William F. Cody earned the nickname "Buffalo Bill" when he was hired in 1867 to supply meat for the men building the Kansas Pacific Railroad through eastern Colorado. With sixty million American bison roaming the Great Plains, buffalo (as we often call them) were a plentiful target. During one seventeen month period, Cody killed more than four thousand bison.

By the early 1870s, the buffalo slaughter reached one million animals a year. By 1895 this great American beast was nearly extinct, and the government stepped in to stop the slaughter. Today some Colorado ranchers raise buffalo, but no longer do millions of the grand creatures roam free with the deer and the antelope.

When buffalo hunting came to an end, Bill Cody organized his Wild West performances. The entertainment included wild beasts, bands of Indians, cowboys, and cowgirls—among them Annie Oakley. Buffalo Bill's Wild West toured the United States and Europe.

When Buffalo Bill died in 1917, he was buried on Lookout Mountain near Golden. His grave was covered with thirty tons of concrete to make certain that the rival town of Cody, Wyoming, would not steal his body for burial there.

Valley, is so arid that it is almost a desert. For nearly 150 years this valley has been home to many Hispanics.

THE WESTERN SLOPE

The Colorado Plateau covers parts of four western states: Colorado, Utah, Arizona, and New Mexico. In fact, at the Four Corners Monument in southwestern Colorado, you can put one hand in

"Cody was a good man who we all loved and respected. He'd give you a nickel of his last dime," said Goldie Griffith Cameron, one of five lady bronco riders in Buffalo Bill's "Wild West."

Utah and one in Colorado, one foot in Arizona, the other in New Mexico—the only point in the United States where you can be in four states at once!

It took millions of years for nature to build the Colorado Plateau. When the Rocky Mountains were pushed up from inside the earth, the plateau lifted up with them. Unlike the plains, where the rock sloped down from the mountains, the plateau remained flat. Even so, this region is called the "Western Slope."

Western Colorado is less densely populated than the Front Range, and the lifestyle here is generally slower. The region's two largest cities, Grand Junction in the center and Durango in the southwest, are small compared to Front Range cities. The plateau is much drier than the rest of the state, but fruit orchards thrive here. Peach grower Earl Brown explains his success: "The Palisade Cliffs and the Grand Mesa Towers and the mountains to the east all hold the daytime heat and keep the temperature at night warm enough for the trees to grow. That warm draft is even called the peach wind." But the mild climate that makes fruit grow so well has also attracted many people; the Western Slope is now in the midst of a population boom.

The Colorado Plateau is rich in minerals. One of the most important is the oil found in shale, a rock that splits easily into thin leaves. Oil shale is a source of fuel. Uranium is another type of fuel buried in the plateau. Nuclear power is produced by splitting its atoms. Vanadium, often found near uranium, is an element used to harden steel. And wherever there is oil, deposits of coal and natural gas are often found.

It's no mystery why the plateau is so rich in fuels. The Western Slope was once home to massive dinosaurs. One hundred and fifty million years ago, the area had a warm, wet climate, with trees like those you might find in a jungle today. Fossils—bones and prints from prehistoric times—have left clues as to what life was like in Colorado long ago. Coal, oil, and natural gas are called "fossil fuels" because they were created from plant and animal remains during the dinosaur era.

North of Grand Junction is Dinosaur National Monument, once

At Dinosaur National Monument, on the Colorado-Utah border, fossils of fourteen different kinds of dinosaurs have been found.

populated by huge vegetarians like brontosaurus, diplodocus, stegosaurus, and their meat-eating enemy allosaurus. At Dinosaur Quarry in the park, scientists are continually uncovering new fossils. One wall, which is enclosed for viewing, displays some 1,600 dinosaur bones.

WEIRD WEATHER

Because it is far from any large body of water, Colorado tends to be quite dry. Nearly every summer afternoon, however, people can expect a thunderstorm, often with tornado warnings, on the eastern plains and along the Front Range. During the winter a

LAND AND WATER

Holyoke

Yuma

Sterling

Fort Morgan

Burlington

Cheyenne Wells

Lamar

Arikaree R.

John Martin Reservoir

Big Sandy R.

La Junta

Purgatoire R.

South Platte R.

Greeley

Denver

Aurora

Colorado Springs

Rocky Ford

Walsenburg

Trinidad

Pueblo

Canon City

Fort Collins

Loveland

Longmont

Boulder

Westminster

Arvada

Lakewood

South Platte R.

Leadville

Salida

Alamosa

Rio Grande R.

Monte Vista

Steamboat Springs

Colorado R.

Yampa R.

Mt. Elbert
(14,433 ft)

Gunnison

Blue Mesa Reservoir

Glenwood Springs

North Fork R.

Craig

Rifle

White R.

Yampa R.

Delta

Montrose

San Miguel R.

Durango

Navajo Reservoir

Cortez

McPhee Reservoir

Grand Junction

"stockman's advisory" warns ranchers of danger to livestock from blizzards.

Colorado's climate is moderate: Temperatures are neither extremely hot nor cold, but they can be very surprising. Snow has fallen in August, and the thermometer can reach 72 degrees Fahrenheit in January. The Chinook is a warm winter wind, which locals call a "snow eater." In a chinook, cold, wet air west of the mountains is pushed up and over the peaks. Near the top the air drops its moisture in the form of snow, which warms the air. A warm wind rushes down the eastern slope at great speeds—more than one hundred miles per hours at times—melting the snow below.

Weather stations in Colorado often report "upslope conditions"— when air moves *up* the sides of the mountains instead of down. The mix of air masses during upslope conditions can bring heavy precipitation. "Hail Alley," which runs roughly along the Front Range, receives more hail than anywhere else in the United States.

A thick mist called "Cheyenne Fog" is another unusual bit of Colorado weather. This mist often gathers around the high mountain peaks. Pikes Peak has Cheyenne Fog about every third day, yet below in Colorado Springs there is fog only twelve days a year.

With its weird weather, desolate plains, and awesome mountains, the settlement of Colorado was left to the strong-hearted. On his first visit west in 1870, Horace Greeley, editor of the New York Tribune, proclaimed, "We seem to have reached the acme of barrenness and desolation." But like many newcomers, Greeley eventually fell in love with the state. He returned with a group of pioneers to found the Union Colony where the city of Greeley now

"It appears that it will never be feasible for the grizzly bear to return to the state." —the Colorado Division of Wildlife

stands. Back home, he urged his readers, "Go West, young man, go West."

ENDANGERED IN COLORADO

"When the grizzly is gone," wrote John McGuire of *Outdoor Life*, "we shall have lost the [noblest] specimen of wildlife [in] the western wilderness." Today the Colorado grizzly *is* gone. Like other endangered animals, the grizzly found it impossible to coexist with the growing numbers of human beings. Other animals, such as the gray wolf, the lynx, and the wolverine, have nearly disappeared.

Fish are also victims of Colorado's growth. Squawfish—known to reach six feet and weigh eighty pounds—have become endangered by the damming of the Colorado River. This, along with pollution caused by industrial and human waste, drastically reduced the numbers of humpback chub, razorback sucker, and green cutthroat trout.

Many great birds that once lived in Colorado became endangered during the twentieth century, their habitats severely reduced or destroyed by people. The peregrine falcon, mascot of the United States Air Force Academy, is endangered but making a comeback, as is the whooping crane and America's national bird, the bald eagle. Through the efforts of the Colorado Department of Wildlife, nesting pairs of these and other endangered birds, such as sandhill cranes, piping plovers, and prairie chickens, have been reintroduced and are starting to breed again.

2 FROM PUEBLOS TO CONDOS

The Chasm of the Colorado, by Thomas Moran

Some of the state's earliest inhabitants roamed the Colorado Plateau hunting animals and gathering nuts and berries. By about A. D. 1 these people were building baskets to hold their food, and so historians call them Basketmakers. These were the first of the Anasazi, whose name in Navajo means "ancient ones."

By A. D. 750 the Anasazi were building their homes from adobe (bricks made from sun-dried mud). In Spanish the word "pueblo" means an adobe village, so these people were called the Pueblo Anasazi. In later years they built their houses under huge sandstone cliffs, which you can see today in Mesa Verde National Park or Hovenweep National Monument.

The Anasazi had left the Four Corners region by A. D. 1300, heading south to mix with other cultures that became known as the Pueblo. Historians don't really know why they left, but a long drought may have been one of the reasons.

FOR GOLD, GOD, AND GLORY

In the 1500s, Spanish conquistadors (conquerors) arrived from Mexico. For more than two hundred years the Spanish came, adventurers in search of gold, missionaries spreading the words of Christ. In 1706, explorer Juan de Ulibarri camped with a party of men near present-day Pueblo. Raising his sword high, Ulibarri

The Cliff Palace at Mesa Verde is, in the words of Colorado historian Frank Waters; "the oldest, largest, and most beautiful monumental ruins in all America."

proclaimed: "In the name of our King, Don Philip V, we claim this land for Spain. Long live the king!"

Contact with the Spanish was very harmful to the Pueblo. The Spanish introduced smallpox, and thousands of Indians died. The Spanish also brought horses to the Pueblo, and soon rival tribes were coming to steal these wonderful creatures. In the battles that followed, the homes and crops of the natives were destroyed. The poorly armed, peaceful Pueblo were no match for the Spanish or the warlike eastern tribes.

EXPLORERS VENTURE WEST AND NORTH

Two Spanish missionaries who traveled through Colorado in 1776 were Fathers Francisco Dominguez and Silvestre Escalante. In his diary Dominguez wrote with enthusiasm, "We proclaimed the Gospel to [the Indians] with such happy results that they are awaiting [other] Spaniards so that they might become Christians."

Thirty years later Zebulon Pike led an exploration party into the region. When he sighted the 14,000-foot mountain that is now named for him, Pike proclaimed, "I believe no man could have ascended to its pinacal [sic]." Today there are auto races up Pikes Peak, and a train takes visitors to the peak's pinnacle several times a day!

During the 1820s and 1830s an adventurous breed of men arrived to trap beaver. Tall hats made of beaver pelts were popular in Europe and America. Trappers could make good money selling pelts to traders, but a mountain man's life was very hard. Trapper Thomas "Broken Hand" Fitzpatrick wrote in his diary about drinking from a buffalo wallow when his group ran out of water: "When the rain falls it is collected in these places and here the buffalo come to drink and stand during the heat of the day, adding their own excrements to the already [rotten] waters."

When the beaver hat craze died out in the mid-1830s, white men

Zebulon Montgomery Pike, explorer and U.S. Army officer. Pike led a party into the Front Range of the Rockies and discovered the peak later named after him. He was killed in battle while leading troops as brigadier general during the War of 1812.

began trading with the Indians for buffalo robes and other hand-crafted items. They set up trading posts and forts where Indians came to trade for beads and trinkets, knives and kettles, powder and lead for their guns. Bent's Fort was a famous trading post on the Santa Fe Trail in southeastern Colorado. Today it is a national historical site near the town of La Junta. At Christmas, modern-day mountain men gather at the fort to reenact an 1840s celebration.

THE UTE, ARAPAHO, AND CHEYENNE

Among the Indian tribes that made the highly prized buffalo robes were the Cheyenne. Like the Arapaho, their neighbors to the north, the Cheyenne made good use of every part of the animal—for food, clothing, tools, weapons, and household supplies. These Plains tribes lived in tepees, performed the Sun Dance, and kept the sacred pipe as part of their rituals.

At the Sun Dance, a young boy would make a very painful sacrifice. He might ask the medicine man to make two cuts in the skin of his chest. Into them were stuck sharp pieces of wood with rope on the ends. After the medicine man tied the rope to a center pole, the boy started dancing. If he did not dance hard enough to tear the wood from his own skin, the medicine man would cut it out.

In the mountains lived the Utes, one of the tribes that stole horses from the Pueblo. Horses made buffalo hunts in the plains much easier and enabled the Utes to defend themselves from their enemies, the Plains Indians. The Arapaho believed their god Manitou ("Man Above") had put up the Rocky Mountains as a fence between their people and the Utes.

An even greater threat to the Utes was the white man. Before 1868, 80 percent of what is now Colorado belonged to the Utes. By 1873 their lands measured less than a third of the state. But the Utes weren't the only ones whose territory was shrinking. To all Colorado natives the settlers were a common enemy.

THE RUSH TO COLORADO

What drew these settlers to Colorado was the discovery of gold by prospector Green Russell and his brothers in 1858. GOLD IN KANSAS! screamed the headline in the *Kansas City* paper. (At the time Colorado was part of Kansas Territory.) "Every man has gold

On the Platte River Near Denver, 1865, *by Worthington Whittredge*

on the tongue, if none in his pocket. . . . If there is not a [decline] in this feeling before spring, our city will be depopulated."

William Larimer, a town promoter, was among the first to arrive. He founded a settlement where Cherry Creek meets the Platte River and named it in honor of James W. Denver, Governor of Kansas Territory. Doctors, shopkeepers, and businesspeople were quick to follow.

In the fall of 1859, Denver's first school opened. That same year the *Rocky Mountain News* printed its first issue. Also in 1859, Clark

ROOT HOG, OR DIE

When word of the discovery of gold around Pikes Peak filtered back east in spring 1859, a great surge of people hit the trail for the Colorado hills. Very few of them struck it rich. The enthusiastic PIKES PEAK OR BUST! signs that the miners had painted on their wagons, had to be painted over with the mournful: BUSTED, BY GOSH!

The expression "root hog, or die" was a way of saying "work hard, or else!"

So we traveled across the country, and we got upon the ground,
But cold weather was ahead, the first thing we found.
We built our shanties on the ground, resolved in spring to try,
To gather up the dust and slugs, root hog, or die.

Speculation is the fashion even at this early stage,
And corner lots and big hotels appear to be the rage.
The emigrations bound to come, and to greet them we will try,
Big pig, little pig, root hog, or die.

Let shouts resound, the cup pass 'round, we all came for gold,
The politicians are all gas, the speculators sold.
The "scads" are all we want, and to get them we will try,
Big pig, little pig, root hog, or die.

Surveyors now are at their work, laying off the towns,
And some will be of low degree, and some of high renown.
They don't care a jot nor little who do buy
The corner lots, or any lots, root hog, or die.

The doctors are among us, you can find them where you will,
They say their trade it is to cure, I say it is to kill;
They'll dose you and they'll physic you, until they make you sigh,
And their powders and their lotions make you root hog, or die.

The next in turn comes lawyers, a precious set are they,
In the public dairy they drink the milk, their clients drink the whey.
A cunning set these fellows are, they'll sap you till you're dry,
And never leave you will they have to root hog, or die.

I have finished now my song, or if you please, my ditty,
And that it was not shorter is about the only pity.
And now that I have had my say, don't say I've told a lie,
For the subject I've touched will make us root hog, or die.

and Gruber established a mint to make coins from the gold. Banks and town governments were set up in Boulder, Denver, and the Pikes Peak region, along with shops, saloons, and services of all sorts. Aunt Clara Brown, a former black slave, opened the first laundry in the state by taking in miners' washing at her cabin in Central City. The region was growing like a prairie wildfire, and on February 28, 1861, Colorado became a territory separate from Kansas.

To haul supplies in and ore out of the mines, prospectors used ox-drawn wagons. But these were small and slow. What the infant territory needed were railroads, and during the next decade, transportation pioneers like William Jackson Palmer, David Moffat, and

A rare tintype of a miner during the 1859 "Pikes Peak or Bust" gold rush.

During 1865, the year this picture was taken in Denver, 62,500 tons of freight were carried into Colorado by these "ships of the prairies."

Otto Mears worked to build them. Palmer's Denver & Rio Grande Western Railroad ran for more than 120 years, and Moffat's ingenious tunnel under the Continental Divide is still used by railroads today.

A DEATH SONG

Railroads brought the Indian conflict to the breaking point. Cheyenne Chief Roman Nose spoke for all the tribes when he warned: "We will not have the wagons which make a noise [railroads] in the hunting grounds of the buffalo. If the palefaces come farther into our land, there will be scalps of your brethren in the wigwams of the Cheyennes."

By the 1860s the Plains Indians had given up so much land in treaties with the white man that they had no place to hunt and no way to feed themselves. Government officials promised to protect the Indians and to pay them for their lands, but this rarely happened. Desperate to feed themselves, the Indians began stealing food and supplies from white settlers.

On the morning of November 29, 1864, a United States Army unit led by Colonel John Chivington—also a Methodist preacher—attacked a settlement of peaceful Cheyenne and Arapaho. They were camped at Sand Creek in southeastern Colorado, a place they had been told was under the protection of the United States government. During the attack, White Antelope, a Cheyenne who had convinced his tribe to trust the whites, "stood in front of his lodge with his arms folded across his breast, singing the death song: 'Nothing lives long, only the earth and the mountains.' "

The Sand Creek Massacre, which killed 10 army volunteers and 150 Indians, was only one of several battles. In the mountains, Indian agent Nathan Meeker was trying to teach the Utes how to live like white people and keep the peace. But the Utes didn't want to change their ways, and in 1879 they revolted, killing Meeker and his men. Newspaper headlines cried THE UTES MUST GO! Many Utes were forced out of their Colorado homeland into Utah. Their descendants now live on reservations in Utah and in southwestern Colorado.

Today's Native American artists remember the past in the designs

"Many non-Indians do not realize how strongly most Indians want to remain Indian," writes J. D. Hughes in American Indians in Colorado

of their jewelry, in paintings, and on pottery. One of the major festivals honoring western and Indian artists is the Colorado Indian Market & Western Art Roundup, held in mid-January in Denver. Here some four hundred artists gather for three days to show and sell their work. In March, Native American artists and craftspeople display their works, and vendors sell native foods at the Denver powwow. Hundreds of dancers and musicians from some seventy tribes around the country come to celebrate their many cultures.

CHIEF OURAY AND CHIPETA

Ouray, whose Indian name means "arrow," was the peace-loving chief of Colorado's Uncompahgre Utes. Unlike many Indian leaders, Ouray realized it was useless for his people to fight the United States government. He worked for treaties that would benefit the Utes, traveling twice to Washington, D.C., to meet with the President.

In 1859 he married Chipeta, a Ute whose name means "White Singing Bird." Chipeta had a lovely voice and later learned to play the guitar. Ouray often listened to Chipeta's advice while he worked for peace with the white man. But as the government broke more and more treaties, Ouray became discouraged and angry. When people asked why he didn't fight he said, "The treaty that an Indian makes with the United States is like the treaty a buffalo makes with his hunters when he has been hit by arrows. All he can do is lie down and give in."

When Ouray learned of the Meeker Massacre in 1879, he gave up the idea

Chipeta

of peace and was ready to fight. Some people say it was only Chipeta's tears that made him change his mind and agree to peace. The next year, although he was very sick, Ouray made one more trip to Washington. The government wanted the Utes to sign a treaty agreeing to move to Utah. It was then that the great Ute chief made his famous statement. "I will never leave my Shining Mountains," he told American leaders. He didn't. He died in August, one month before the papers were signed that forced the Utes to move to a reservation in Utah.

The Bear Dance, where Ouray met and fell in love with Chipeta, is still held on the Southern Ute Reservation. "Leave your troubles behind and start your life anew," is the motto of this festival. It is held in the spring to wake up the natives, just the way bears emerge from hibernation. The dance is led by Ute women, who later ask the men to join them. Dancers sway to the music like large, sleepy bears.

"Is not the United States government strong enough to keep its treaties?"
—Ute Chief Ouray

THE CENTENNIAL STATE

On August 1, 1876, Colorado became the thirty-eighth state. Because this was exactly one hundred years after America's independence, Colorado is called the Centennial State. Each year Coloradans celebrate August 1 as Colorado Day. But the one hundredth Colorado Day celebration in 1976 was marked by a tragic event. In the afternoon of July 31, a thunderstorm stalled over the Big Thompson canyon near Loveland. Twelve inches of rain poured into the canyon in just a few hours. Flash floods killed 145 people in Colorado's worst natural disaster.

Gold, Silver, and Coal. Mining was at first the biggest business in the Centennial State, but agriculture soon took hold on the eastern plains. Pioneers learned how to raise corn, wheat, and other crops in the "Great American Desert." Some settled independently; others organized "agricultural colonies" like those in Greeley and Longmont.

From 1870 to 1880, Colorado's population increased from nearly 40,000 to 200,000. Gold was not the only attraction. Silver brought thousands of miners to places like Aspen and Creede. In Leadville, storekeeper H. A. W. Tabor became fantastically wealthy by "grubstaking" two poor miners. He gave them food and supplies in exchange for a share of whatever silver they found. The two struck a rich vein in the Little Pittsburgh Mine, which a year later was worth $20 million.

Another Leadville miner, Jim Brown, also struck it rich in silver. But it was his wife, Margaret, who became famous as the Unsinkable Molly Brown when she helped save passengers trapped on

REMEMBERING DAYS GONE BY

If you're wondering what it would have been like to live through the Colorado Gold Rush, go to Idaho Springs, west of Denver, in July. During Gold Rush Days there are mucking contests where would-be miners challenge each other to load broken rock into ore carts by hand. They also compete in jackhammer drilling contests. Spectators pan for gold, pitch horseshoes, and swing picks and axes like old-time prospectors.

To relive the heyday of silver mining, go to Leadville in early August. For one weekend, hardrock miners roam the sidewalks, dance hall girls perform in the saloons, and brass bands parade in the streets. Boom Days concludes with a burro race to the top of nearby Mosquito Pass. Local people challenge each other to "Get Your Ass Over the Pass."

the *Titanic*, the ship that sank in 1912 on its first trans-Atlantic voyage. Yelled Molly to one of the *Titanic*'s owners who tried to save himself before the women and children, "In Leadville, Colorado, where I come from, you would be strung up on the nearest pine tree."

Leadville, like most boom towns, was "ramshackle, rough, dirty, boisterous and devil-may-care," wrote Colorado historian Caroline Bancroft, "but remarkably honest. . . . Despite the fact that tents and cabins [the miners' homes] had no doors, there was almost no thievery." The laws were simple: no claim jumping, stealing, or murder. Anything else was okay.

A Leadville miner uses a "rocker" to wash the metal ore free from the rock.

Goldseeker Winfield Scott Stratton was drawn to the southern gold fields of the Pikes Peak region where he spent twenty summers looking for a "strike." In 1891 it happened at Cripple Creek, and overnight Stratton became one of the richest men in Colorado. Most prospectors never got that lucky. They spent what little they made in the saloons and gambling houses. Dance hall girls like Mattie Silks and her ladies entertained the miners at night. During the day, con artists like Soapy Smith played "confidence" games on people, tricking them into taking chances on games that were rigged so only Smith and his men would win. In the mining town of Creede, the editor of the *Chronicle* wrote in a poem, "It's day all day in the daytime, And there is no night in Creede."

At the start of the twentieth century, many Colorado men were coal miners. Most of them worked long hours for low pay. In the hope of improving their situation, many miners began to strike. They refused to work until hours were shortened, pay was increased, or conditions in the mines were made safer. The strikes caused friction with mine owners, and in several places the National Guard was called in to bring labor disputes under control.

War and Industry. When America entered World War I in 1917, Colorado farmers found their products in great demand. The army needed large quantities of sugar beets, wheat, potatoes, and beans. But when the war ended in 1918 and the demand dropped, the prices of farm products dropped, too. Suddenly farmers found themselves unable to pay their bills and many went bankrupt.

In the 1930s, the entire country sank into the Great Depression. Many Colorado banks and businesses, along with others across the country, failed. When millions of people were unemployed, the government started programs to put people to work. One of the biggest was the Civilian Conservation Corps, which trained young men to build roads and trails in national forests and set up recreational facilities. With so much national forest land in Colorado, the CCC put more than five thousand young people to work.

In 1941, as America entered World War II, Colorado again played an important role. Northwest of Leadville, the army established Camp Hale to train soldiers to fight on skis. This elite group of several thousand rugged men, known as the Tenth Mountain

Division, fought some grueling battles in the mountains of Italy. Toward the end of the war, as the development of the atomic bomb was under way, Colorado became a primary source for two important metals: uranium, used to create an atomic explosion; and plutonium, used in the triggers of atomic bombs.

After the war, the military established important bases around Colorado, among them the U.S. Air Force Academy, built in 1958, and NORAD, the North American Air Defense Command. Many

POPULATION GROWTH: 1870–1990

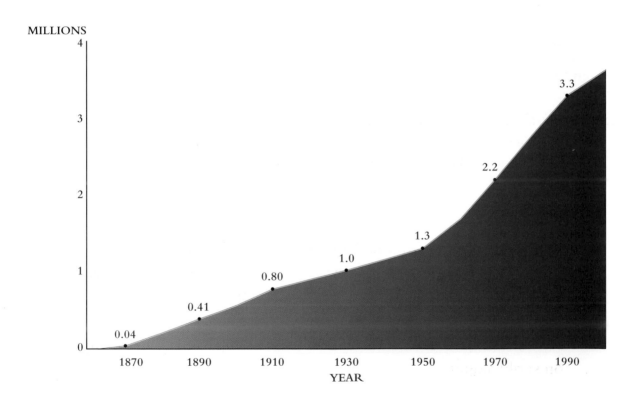

The United States Air Force Academy, north of Colorado Springs, is the state's number one manmade tourist attraction. The first class of cadets graduated in 1959.

of the men who had trained at Camp Hale returned to Colorado's rugged mountains. They helped to start an industry that has become a major source of income for the state: skiing. The resorts that lie nestled today in the Colorado Rockies are a mecca for skiers who are drawn from around the world to that perfect powder run on sunlit slopes.

3 RUNNING THE STATE

Colorado's state capitol in Denver

Government is very big in Colorado, and there are many governments . . . to be exact: 1,936! There is the federal government, the State of Colorado, 63 counties, 267 cities and towns, 176 school districts and 1,428 special districts that oversee everything from local libraries to fire departments.

—*legislative consultant Roger Walton*

Both Denver and Colorado are often called "little Washington." There are more federal government agencies here than in any city or state outside Washington, D.C.

Colorado sends two senators and six representatives to the Congress in Washington, D.C. Pat Schroeder, the state's first female representative, served from 1973 to 1996. Native American Senator Ben Nighthorse Campbell is a colorful figure who rides Harley-Davidson motorcycles and wears traditional Indian garb to political events.

INSIDE GOVERNMENT

The three branches of state government—the executive, legislative, and judicial—are headquartered at the capitol in Denver.

Executive. The executive branch is headed by the governor who

"I've been a policeman, a teacher, a truck driver, a delinquent, a street kid, a farmer, a soldier," said Senator Ben Nighthorse Campbell "A lot of people in public office never had those experiences."

is elected by the people, along with the lieutenant governor, secretary of state, and several other officials. Former Colorado governor Richard Lamm, known nationally for taking unpopular stands on major political issues, made an unsuccessful run for President on the Reform Party ticket in 1996. The executive branch sees that the state's laws are upheld. The laws are based on the Colorado constitution, which was approved on July 1, 1876.

Legislative. The legislative branch, called the general assembly, makes the state's laws. The general assembly has one hundred members, sixty-five in the house of representatives and thirty-five in

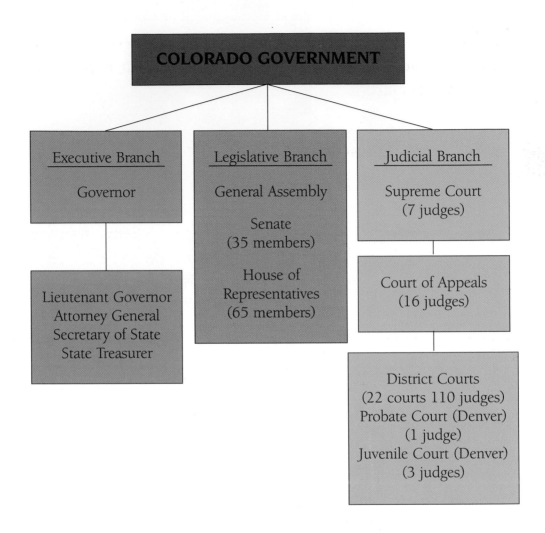

COLORADO GOVERNMENT

Executive Branch

Governor

Lieutenant Governor
Attorney General
Secretary of State
State Treasurer

Legislative Branch

General Assembly

Senate
(35 members)

House of
Representatives
(65 members)

Judicial Branch

Supreme Court
(7 judges)

Court of Appeals
(16 judges)

District Courts
(22 courts 110 judges)
Probate Court (Denver)
(1 judge)
Juvenile Court (Denver)
(3 judges)

the senate. Representatives decide how the state will raise and spend its money.

Judicial. The judicial branch is made up of many courts, with one or more appointed judges presiding over each. It is the job of the courts to explain the laws and be certain they uphold the Colorado Constitution. When a person disagrees with the decision of a judge or jury in one court, he or she can "appeal," or ask a higher court to reconsider the decision. The highest state court is the Colorado Supreme Court, made up of seven justices, one of whom is chief justice.

COUNTY AND LOCAL GOVERNMENTS

Colorado is divided into sixty-three counties, each governed by eight elected officials and a board of at least three elected county commissioners. The commissioners appoint a county attorney.

TEN LARGEST CITIES

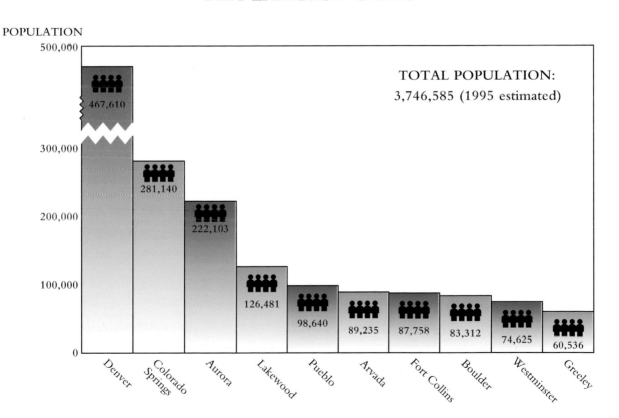

POPULATION

TOTAL POPULATION:
3,746,585 (1995 estimated)

500,000

467,610

300,000

281,140

200,000

222,103

126,481

100,000

98,640

89,235

87,758

83,312

74,625

60,536

0

Denver

Colorado Springs

Aurora

Lakewood

Pueblo

Arvada

Fort Collins

Boulder

Westminster

Greeley

County governments handle construction and maintenance of county roads, health and sanitation, welfare, planning and zoning, licensing, and agriculture and soil conservation.

There are different forms of local governments, but often towns (with two thousand or fewer people) have a mayor and six trustees. The trustees hire or appoint a town manager, police and fire chiefs, and people to handle sewer and water service. Cities may have a council-manager or a mayor-council form of government. In some cities the people elect the mayor; in others the mayor is elected by the council.

Denver's government is different because the city and county are combined. The city limits are also the county limits. Denver has a mayor-council form of government. Former Denver mayor Federico Peña, who told Denverites to "imagine a great city," left his job in 1993, as Denver International Airport was being built, to become Secretary of Transportation under President Bill Clinton.

COLORADO CITIZENS ARE CONCERNED ABOUT . . .

To vote in Colorado, a person must be at least eighteen years old and have been a resident of his or her district for at least twenty-five days. Citizens have not only a right to vote, but a responsibility. "Democracy will not survive as a spectator sport," says government expert Roger Walton.

Drunk Driving. Many Coloradans are upset by the number of accidents that have been caused by drunk drivers in their state. Deaths have jumped 24 percent during the last three years, to a number that the state's transportation safety manager calls, "very

It took six hundred rail car loads of Colorado and Georgia marble to build the City and County Building of Denver's "municipal palace." Each year the building is decorated with twenty thousand colored lights to form the world's largest Christmas lighting display.

worrisome." Says an official of MADD (Mothers Against Drunk Drivers), "I'm devastated." A test is used to determine if a person is driving under the influence (DUI) or driving while intoxicated (DWI). The penalty is determined by the court. First-time offenders may be fined, sentenced to jail, made to do community service, or may have their driver's licenses suspended or be required to enter a rehabilitation program.

Education. Another issue of major concern is education. More and more parents are upset with the quality of Colorado's schools and with social issues their kids face there. Because Colorado requires that children age seven to sixteen must be educated, many parents are turning to home schooling. When kids are schooled at home, they must be taught for at least four hours a day and study subjects approved by the state.

Charter schools, which are organized privately but operate on school district funds, are also growing in number. The charter, which states guidelines the school will follow, must be approved by the local school board. "It's been a great alternative for us," says one parent from the Academy of Charter Schools. "The emphasis is on basics: reading, writing, math. Teachers don't spend a lot of time teaching about moral issues—things the kids should be learning at home."

Colorado got some bad publicity in 1992 when voters approved Amendment No. 2. This amendment would have stopped local governments from passing laws to protect homosexuals against discrimination. Certain groups were so angered they declared a boycott against Colorado, refusing to sell Colorado products or hold their conventions here. In 1996 the United States Supreme

Court struck down the amendment, saying it violated the U.S. Constitution.

Gambling. In 1990, Colorado voters approved gambling in Central City, Black Hawk, and Cripple Creek. Today more than sixty casinos are in operation. Gambling brings nearly half a billion dollars a year to the state. But it also brings congestion, traffic, and crime to the tiny mountain towns. The Colorado Senate

In the heyday of gold mining, Central City was known as "the richest square mile on earth." Today it is rich with gamblers spending their money in the casinos.

On high pollution days, especially in winter, Denver's "brown cloud" obscures the downtown skyline.

recently approved a bill to keep children out of casinos. "I've seen children sleeping on the floor or carrying tubs of nickels for their parents," said sponsor Joan Johnson. The Casino Owners Association of Colorado supports the measure.

Air Pollution. Sixth grader Valerie Martinez, like millions of Coloradans, worries about air pollution. "When you wake up in the mornings, sometimes you can see a red fog and that's pollution." Clean Air Colorado is an agency that educates people about air pollution. It tests cars to see that their emissions are not causing pollution. During the high pollution season (November 1 through March 31) Clean Air Colorado issues air quality reports twice a day. A blue pollution advisory means the air quality is good. A red advisory means Denver metro residents cannot burn wood in stoves or fireplaces and should limit their driving.

Crime. In a recent eight-year period, the number of arrests for violent crimes among teenagers increased by 72 percent. Colorado's crime rate is a little better than average in the United States; the state ranks twenty-first out of fifty. But many young people feel that's way too high. Says Andrea Flores, "The thing I dislike most about living in Colorado is the guns, fighting, and people that are prejudiced." Fred Price agrees: "I don't like the gangs around Denver because I can't even go out my front door without wondering if I'll be shot."

Politicians are taking steps to curb Colorado's violent crime rate. In a 1996 letter to the *Denver Post*, Governor Roy Romer, Representative Patricia Schroeder, Denver mayor Wellington Webb, and Aurora mayor Paul Tauer shared their plans for a project called PACT: Pulling America's Communities Together. The focus of the project, they explained, was on juvenile violence. "But we know the roots of that violence lie elsewhere: in our media, our schools, our neighborhoods and our homes." They promised to put new effort into programs such as curfew enforcement and finding jobs for young people. "If we all do our part," they concluded, "we can get to the heart of the problem of juvenile violence [and have] another peaceful Summer of Safety."

HOW COLORADANS EARN A LIVING

In 1995, *Denver Post* business columnist Alex Berenson wrote, "Colorado's economy almost ran off the tracks." Business profits were down and growth in the state had slowed. But, says Tucker Hart Adams, chief economist for Colorado National Bank, "I think the worst of the slowdown is over." Telecommunications and retail trade are among the industries that will lead Colorado's growth in the late 1990s. Other major contributions to the state's economy are mining, agriculture, tourism, and technology.

Mining. Mining is still an important part of Colorado's economy. After World War II, when the demand for oil increased, companies began drilling in eastern Colorado and processing shale on the Western Slope. As nuclear energy came into wider use, energy companies required uranium. Nearly three-fourths of the world's molybdenum (ma-LIB-den-um) is mined in Colorado. "Moly" is used with iron to make high-speed cutting tools.

Agriculture. Many Coloradans are also employed in farming and ranching. In 1995, Coloradans Tom and Shawn Edwards celebrated a century of farming on the Edwards' family land ."My family always raised wheat and corn for the cattle, and they always had cattle," recalls Tom. At a time when it is harder than ever to earn a living farming, the Edwards have shown a lot of determination. Tom credits new methods of crop rotation, tilling, and fertilizing. But Shawn says it's advice from Tom's grandmother that has made this family business successful. "She always told us if you keep your family as the top priority, everything else will fall into place; the rest is just icing on the cake."

Field crops like grains and beans, corn, hay, wheat, and potatoes create the most agricultural income for Colorado. Nearly all the potatoes raised in Weld, the largest agricultural county, are made into potato chips. San Luis Valley farmer Jerry Smith, chairman of the National Potato Promotion Board, hopes to see this Colorado product used in fast food restaurants around the world.

Onions are Colorado's biggest small-farm vegetable crop, and the state ranks third in the nation for numbers of onions raised. Another "best" are the incredibly sweet, juicy cantaloupes raised near Rocky Ford in southeastern Colorado. The town, which calls

Hay and wheat are both big crops in Colorado. "We raise too much and the price is too low. Raise too little and we lose money," says Irwin Casper, a Colorado rancher's son. "There has to be a future in the land, but it sure isn't easy."

FUN-FILLED COLORADO FAIRS

The "Fun and Only" Colorado State Fair has taken place in Pueblo every August since 1872. Today it draws more than a million visitors a year, making it the thirteenth largest in the nation. The fair runs for eleven days. During that time there are three parades and seven days of rodeos, sponsored by the Professional Rodeo Cowboys Association. The fair has all kinds of high-tech exhibits and agricultural displays with Western themes. The small animal competition includes the world's largest rabbit show. There's also a stock show, a fiesta, world-class carnival rides, and contests for kids in bubble gum blowing and melon racing. The State Fair also offers big-name entertainment, usually by country western musicians.

The city of Denver also hosts two large fairs. In late May is the

Capitol Hill People's Fair. This twenty-five-year-old event draws three hundred thousand visitors, who stroll among the six hundred or more booths that offer everything from exotic food to intricate crafts to advice on sewing or politics. The Festival of Mountain and Plain has been held in Denver since 1895. Its main attraction is the Taste of Colorado, where some of the finest restaurants feature free samples from their menus.

itself the nation's melon capital, claims that 95 percent of the world's cantaloupe seed is grown on its farms.

Brilliant sunshine and mild temperatures make Colorado a major supplier of carnations. Greenhouses—of which there are fewer and fewer as the cost of natural gas rises—produce carnations in brilliant colors that stay fresh for weeks in a vase after being cut.

Sheep and cattle are the most common Colorado livestock, raised on ranches in the eastern plains or in the mountain parks. Stockmen operate feedlots where the animals are sent to be fattened before they are slaughtered. In fact, Colorado has more sheep and lamb in feedlots than any other state. Monfort of Colorado is the biggest cattle feeder in the United States

If you like turkey bologna or turkey hot dogs you can thank the big birds raised in Colorado. Some do end up on Thanksgiving platters, but many more are shipped to food processing companies like Longmont Foods to be packaged with some other meat form, such as ham or hamburger.

Technology. In recent years, Colorado's Front Range has become a high-tech center. Computer giants like Hewlett Packard, Storage Technology, IBM, and DEC (Digital Equipment Corporation) have national or regional headquarters here. "Programming, data processing and other related services—including software—are on a roll," reports the *Denver Post*.

Big companies are attracted to Colorado because it's a beautiful place to live and work. "We'd been here as plain old postcard buying tourists," recalled the wife of a U.S. West employee. "When my husband had the chance to transfer here we couldn't believe it. It didn't take long to say yes."

Tourism. With all its natural beauty, it's not surprising that tourism is one of the top ten businesses in Colorado. More than 60,000 people work in tourist-related fields, serving the 20 million or more travelers who visit Colorado each year. Many come in the summer to hike or camp in the mountains. But the big-money attraction is skiing. Resorts like Breckenridge, Keystone, Steamboat Springs, Winter Park, and twenty other ski areas, attract more than ten million people each year. A *Skiing* magazine survey of favorite ski resorts worldwide, chose Colorado for three of its top ten: Vail, Aspen, and Telluride. "Aspen is a place," wrote columnist Hollis Brooks, "where most people ski to be seen." Not all resorts are so fashion conscious. Vail is a place for all ages, "like a big city compris[ed] of many neighborhoods that you can sample day by day," says one visitor. The cowboy ski town of Steamboat Springs is "down-home, all-American, blue-jeans friendly," writes *Skiing's* Eric Hanson. "Cowboy hats and boots are as common as powder

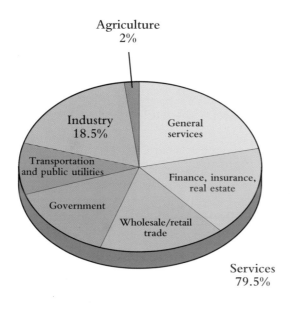

Agriculture
2%

Industry
18.5%

General
services

Transportation
and public utilities

Finance, insurance,
real estate

Government

Wholesale/retail
trade

Services
79.5%

1992 GROSS STATE PRODUCT: $82 BILLION

EARNING A LIVING

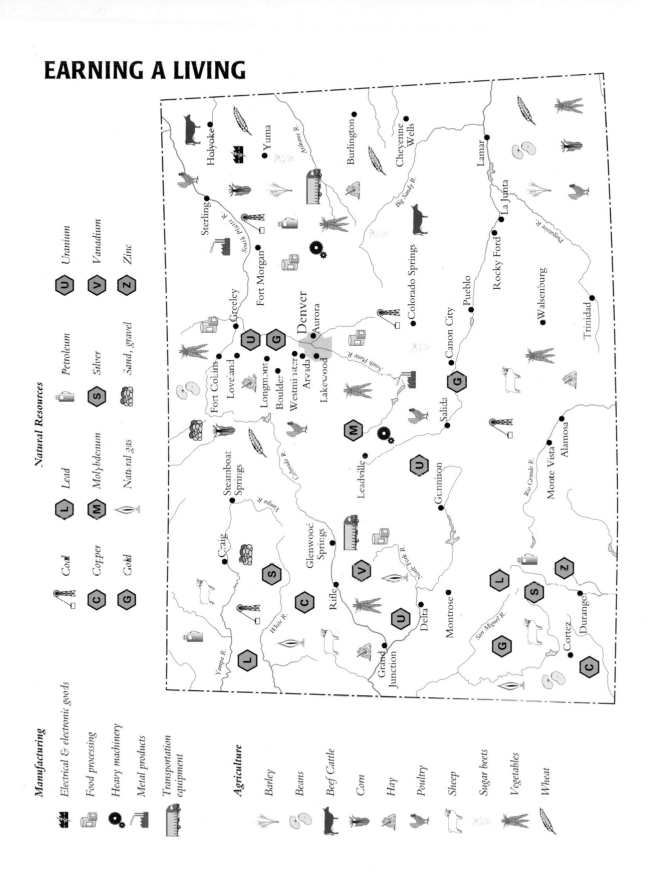

suits and ski boots. . . . The mountain itself is about as kid-friendly as you can get. "

In addition to the best skiing in North America, Colorado ski resorts sponsor special events to lure tourists. Each January Breckenridge hosts the Ullrfest and World Cup Freestyle in honor of Ull, the Norse god of winter. Along with a parade and fireworks, there are Nordic events and a freestyle skiing competition with some of the world's best.

The Steamboat Springs Winter Carnival runs for a week in February and features ice sculpture competitions, a hockey tournament, and ski jumping. There's also a race, in which riders sit on shovels and are pulled by horses through the streets. The high school band marches on skis, and at night a "lighted man" skis down nearby Howelsen Hill. The scene is similar at Winterskol, where fireworks and torchlight runs draw onlookers out into the night at Snowmass and Aspen.

"Colorado's mountains are the best in the country," says Loveland ski instructor Shawn O'Hara. "I've taught at a bunch of areas, you'll never find anything like the superb powder, the high-altitude sun, the gorgeous blue sky, and the friendly, laid-back people in this state."

Telluride. The Colorado ski industry has come a long way since the state's first rope tow was installed on Berthoud Pass in 1937.

4 LIVING THE GOOD LIFE

To see the mix of ethnic groups that make up Colorado, look at a map of Denver. Major streets like Larimer, Gilpin, and Evans, were named for white settlers. Native American names appear from A to Z: Acoma to Zuni. Colorado's Hispanic heritage is remembered in street names like Tejon, Umatilla, and Santa Fe. Black leaders from Martin Luther King to "Daddy" Bruce Randolph—the barbecue chef who fed Denver's poor and homeless each Thanksgiving—have major Denver streets in their names. In downtown Denver is Sakura Square, a center for Japanese shops.

HISPANIC COLORADO TODAY

The state's oldest permanent town, San Luis, was founded in 1851 by Hispanic settlers from New Mexico. The region became the center of Colorado's Hispanic culture, and Hispanic traditions are very much alive here today. Sheepherders follow their flocks, and women weave beautiful fabrics from wool. Grandparents pass on their Hispanic heritage by telling children *cuentos*—Hispanic stories or folk tales.

Colorado Latinos also enjoy singing *alabados*, or ballads, Spanish folk songs that tell a story. In *Agraciada Golondrina*, "Graceful Swallow," a young man gives a letter to a swallow, asking the bird to deliver it to his girlfriend, who is far away. In three days

In the largely Hispanic San Luis Valley, Catholics have built churches and shrines to their holy figures, such as this portrayal of Christ falling beneath the weight of the cross.

the bird returns with a message: the young man must console himself with the bird cage, because the bird has flown away.

Hispanic Coloradans also sing *corridos*, songs the cowboys sang while they drove cattle from Texas north to Kansas or Colorado. Most, such as *El Vaquero* (the cowboy), deal with hardship, violence, or tragedy:

> When we drove out toward Kansas
> With that bunch of rangy steers
> Wow! What troubles we endured
> Driving through those endless plains!

A HISPANIC CUENTO: THREE PIECES OF GOOD ADVICE

Long ago, three poor men on the road ran into a rich man who had three bags of money. "I will give you each one of these bags," said the man, "OR I will give you three pieces of good advice." Two of the men took the money. The third took the advice:

1. *Do not go down strange roads.*
2. *Mind your own business.*
3. *Look before you leap.*

The men with the money headed home on a strange road that they thought would be quicker, but thieves attacked them, stole their money, and killed them. The third man stayed on the familiar road until he came to a farmhouse where he was invited for supper. Here he noticed that the farmer's wife was very thin, but he asked no questions. For several days he stayed and worked on the farm. When he was ready to leave the farmer said to him, "I am very rich and I am going to give you all my money." The man was flabbergasted. "Why me?" he asked. "Because," said the farmer, "long ago I decided to feed my wife only bones and dry tortillas. I knew she would get very thin and everyone would ask what was wrong. I made up my mind that the first person who did not ask would get all my land and money."

The delighted man rushed home, but when he looked in the window he saw his wife kissing a priest. In a rage, he pulled out his gun, but just in time he remembered, "Look before you leap." Looking again he realized that his wife was kissing their son, who had become a priest while the man was gone!

ETHNIC COLORADO

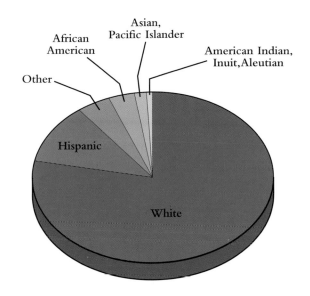

Some of the best Mexican food in the country is cooked in Colorado. Tortillas, round breadlike food, are made from flour or ground corn. Tortillas are the base for tacos, enchiladas, *flautas*, fajitas (say the "j" like "h"), burritos, and other delicious Mexican dishes. Chili peppers, cheese, and *frijoles refritos* (refried beans), along with big dollops of guacamole and sour cream, make great eating!

The Catholic church is the heart of Latino family life. Many churches are decorated with *santos*: paintings and statues of saints. The figures are of two types: *retablos* are pictures of the Holy Family painted on pine boards; *bultos* are statues of religious figures carved out of cottonwood roots.

Many Hispanic festivals—*fiestas*—honor saints in the Catholic church. At many *fiestas* you can find a *piñata*, a clay jar covered with paper, usually formed in an animal shape and filled with candy and goodies. Today many *piñatas* are made of papier-mâché, but the fun is still the same. Children put on blindfolds and try to hit the *piñata* with a stick. When it breaks they scramble to grab the treats.

Other Hispanic holidays celebrate events from the past. On September 16, 1810, Mexicans began a war to break free of Spanish rule. Today Latinos celebrate Mexican Independence Day with parades, speeches, and the waving of Mexican flags. On May 5, 1862, Mexican soldiers won a great victory against French forces, although they were outnumbered three to one. In honor of that victory, Hispanic Coloradans celebrate *Cinco de Mayo* with festivals,

In Greeley, Cinco de Mayo *lasts a full week. Artists, poets, musicians, dancers, teachers, actors, political figures, and others gather to celebrate their Hispanic heritage.*

music, and food fairs. In Denver, more than 120,000 people gather in Civic Center Park to enjoy food, music, and crafts. *Cinco de Mayo* has become much more than a Hispanic holiday. As festival organizer Virginia Martinez says, "The emphasis on this event . . . is to bring *all* races together."

Another Hispanic event enjoyed by millions of westerners is the rodeo. "Rodeo" means "cattle roundup," for it was Mexican cowboys driving their herds into Texas that started these contests on horses. On the long cattle drives, cowboys challenged each other to throw a coiled rope, to ride the wildest bull or horse. Today, rodeos are a symbol of the West. Children, adults, and professional cowboys compete. Pikes Peak or Bust, the state's largest outdoor rodeo, is held in mid-August in Colorado Springs. After the professional event is the National Little Britches Rodeo for kids eight to eighteen. Denver's National Western, the world's largest livestock show, runs for two weeks in January and includes twenty-three rodeos.

But for some Latinos, life in Colorado is neither positive nor promising. Many Hispanic families say the educational system fails their students. Dropout rates are too high; grades and test scores are too low. Of the thirty thousand Latino students in the Denver Public Schools, 10 percent were suspended last year. Only half of all Latino students graduated. "There is a district-wide malaise [illness] in terms of Hispanic student achievement," says advisor Patricio Cordova.

Violence, crime, and gang warfare are major problems in some of Colorado's Hispanic communities. Rival gangs operate within the state, particularly in the Denver area. Sergeant Dennis Cribari

The annual Colorado State Fair in Pueblo features seven days of rodeo events.

In the junior rodeos, it's not always bulls that are ridden! This boy is giving his all in a "mutton bustin'" contest.

of the Denver Police Department's gang unit says violence is bound to result "when you got one gang going into the turf of another gang."

Today many Latinos live outside the San Luis Valley. The largest number live in Denver, followed by Pueblo, Adams, and El Paso counties. Thirteen out of every hundred Coloradans are Hispanic: nearly five hundred thousand in all. Many speak both Spanish and English. It is sometimes said that Latinos have a *mañana* (tomorrow) attitude, meaning that their lifestyle is more relaxed than that of Anglos: what doesn't get done today will get done tomorrow. "We know how to relax, man," laughs twenty-nine-year-old Pat Chavez, "something you gringos have to learn."

THE INDIAN INFLUENCE

Senator Ben Nighthorse Campbell often gets strange looks when he walks into his U.S. Senate office wearing a bolo tie and cowboy boots. When he rode his horse Warbonnet and wore his American Indian headdress in Bill Clinton's inaugural parade, the cameramen hovered around. Why did he do it? "I wanted to let Indian people know they're not forgotten, that we're still here, we're still part of America. . . . I was trying to inspire Indian kids to be aware of it, proud of it, and not forget." Campbell is a Northern Cheyenne whose grandfather was a Sun Dance priest.

Today fewer than 1 percent of Coloradans are Native Americans, but Indian influence on the state is great. In addition to county names such as Kiowa and Cheyenne, mountain peaks like Uncompahgre and Tabeguache, and towns named Ouray and Saguache;

"It is important to us to keep the traditions of our fathers."
—Ute Mountain Ute tribal member

Indian crafts, foods, and ways of thinking are a large part of Colorado life.

There is not as much poverty on Colorado's Indian reservations as there is on some other reservations in the nation. Oil and gas reserves on reservation lands provide income for the tribes. About one thousand people live on the Southern Ute reservation and another twelve hundred or so on the Ute Mountain Ute reservation. Both tribes are known for their talented craftsmen. The Sky Ute Gallery features exquisite leather and beadwork for which the Southern Utes are famous. The Ute Mountain Utes create pottery using factory-produced clay. Potters form and paint their pieces at the tribe's pottery plant, which is open for tours. Ute pottery is unique for its black-on-white design like that of the Anasazi. But each artist has a distinctive style and every design is one of a kind.

Colorado's Native American jewelers make beautiful silver pieces, often decorated with turquoise or other native stones. In their designs they use Indian symbols such as thunderbirds, turtles, and salamanders.

In many Colorado supermarkets, shoppers can buy Anasazi beans—the very same kind that Colorado's ancient Indians ate for supper two thousand years ago! Another popular Indian food is blue corn chips, made of corn that is actually blue. Ute tortillas are a type of round Indian bread with a flour base that is grilled over an outdoor fire and served with roasted meat, fried potatoes, and green chilis.

Like their ancestors, Colorado Indians are respectful of nature and the environment. They worship many different gods, whom they believe control natural events. Their beliefs are reflected in

Some of Colorado's Native American potters use black-and-white designs like those of the ancient Anasazi.

legends. One legend centers around Mount Shavano, the 14,229-foot peak named for the Ute chief who remained loyal to the United States during the Ute uprising of 1879. In May and early June, when the snow is melting off the high peaks, deep crevices on the east side of Mount Shavano remain filled with snow, making the mountain look like an angel with outstretched wings. The angel is said to have been an Indian princess who misbehaved so badly that the gods turned her to ice and put her on the mountain. One year when the valley was parched by a lack of rain, the princess began to cry. Her tears (the melting snow) saved the people from drought.

FARMERS AND MINERS

Many of Colorado's white settlers were miners who came from Europe, particularly Italy, to work in the "diggings." When the gold

CHEYENNE BATTER BREAD

Before the Cheyenne began hunting buffalo on the Great Plains, they were farmers who lived in villages and grew corn. After the Cheyenne were moved to reservations, they learned to make variations on traditional cornmeal recipes. For the first time they could bake breads and cakes in an oven.

Serves 6

- 1 quart milk or water
- 2 cups yellow or white cornmeal
- 3 eggs, separated
- 4 tablespoons melted butter
- 1-1/2 teaspoons salt
- 1/2 teaspoon pepper

Preheat the oven to 375°. (Ask an adult to help you when using the oven or stove.) Bring milk to a boil in a large saucepan over medium heat. Gradually stir in the cornmeal, stirring for a few minutes until it thickens. Separate the egg whites from the yolks, putting the whites aside in a separate bowl. (This is tricky; you might want an adult to help you crack the first egg.) Beat together the egg yolks, butter, and salt and pepper. In a separate bowl, beat the egg whites until they stand in stiff peaks. Fold the whites into the corn mixture and pour into a 2-quart baking dish. Bake for 20 to 30 minutes, until the bread puffs up and turns golden brown on top. Delicious when served warm with a dab of butter or a little honey.

and silver crazes were over, these immigrants found work in the coal mines along the Front Range and in Routt County. For most, the dream of striking it rich would never come true. "It was a lot of hard work and no money," said Martin Mata who worked in the coal mines in Firestone, Colorado. "We had to load two cars of rock to get one car of coal." For this, recalled Rosario Romano, miners made about three dollars for an eight hour day.

In the late 1800s and early 1900s, German Russian immigrants came to Colorado to homestead and farm. These people had moved from Germany to Russia in the early 1800s to farm new lands. Now their children and grandchildren were moving to Colorado to do the same. Immigrant Charles Boettcher brought sugar beet seeds with him from Germany. Over the years these seeds "grew" into Great Western Sugar, one of the largest sugar companies in the nation.

San Luis Valley farmers discovered irrigation in 1852, but it took

"You think it's unfair I didn't get extra pay for dangerous work? Ha! 'Course it's not fair, but there was a lot of things in the mines that wasn't fair."

—retired coal miner
Genaro deSantis

According to The Colorado Guide, *"In early June, the Cherry Blossom Festival makes [Sakura Square] as crowded as Tokyo at rush hour."*

the German Russians on the eastern plains longer to begin using the technique in raising sugar beets and potatoes. It was the German Russians, says historian Robert Athearn, who did more than any other group to develop farming in eastern Colorado. Another hard-working group were the Japanese immigrants, who triumphed over heat, drought, and plagues of locusts to farm the High Plains. Despite their success—or perhaps because of it—

other workers resented the Japanese. Then, during World War II, many Japanese Americans were seen as a threat to national security and housed in Colorado "relocation camps" (like prisons). Despite this long history of prejudice, today the Japanese own many of eastern Colorado's largest garden farms.

These large farms would not have thrived without Mexican field workers who arrived shortly after 1900. "There was a demand for cheap, easily managed 'stoop' labor," writes Athearn. "German Russians . . . were not the answer because they [became] growers, rather than laborers; the same was true of the Japanese." Because there were few jobs in Mexico, thousands of Latinos came north, in search of work hoeing, weeding, and harvesting the huge fields.

Soon the U.S. government put a limit on the number who could come. Still, life here offered so much more than in Mexico that people continued to stream across the border. Immigration has become a heated issue in Colorado today. "Many [Coloradans] recognize that there is an [illegal alien] problem and that it is growing more disturbing every day," says Tom Tancredo, president of a research firm that studies social problems. "Colorado taxpayers must ante up tens of millions of dollars every year to provide services for aliens."

Others feel that in spite of the cost, it is wrong for America to close its borders. After all, they say, ours is a nation built by immigrants. Denver native Linda Chavez, president of the Center for Equal Opportunity, strongly opposes cutting the current level of legal immigration. If that happens, she says, "many immigrants who occupy [low-skilled or manual labor] jobs will disappear from the economy, with perhaps disastrous consequences."

COWBOYS, YOUNG PROFESSIONALS, AND SKI BUMS

About 80 percent of Coloradans are Anglos, representing lifestyles from briefcase-carrying lawyers and oil company executives to hardrock miners. On the eastern plains and the Western Slope are the cowboys—rough, tough, weather-beaten men and hard-working women who drive pickup trucks, wear cowboy boots and hats, and are generally conservative in their thinking. Colorado also has its share of "urban cowboys"—city dwellers who look and dress like working cowboys.

Many Colorado Anglos are single, under fifty, well educated, and career-minded. "This is a place where you can stay forever young," says thirty-nine-year-old Kirstin Karsch, a Denver attorney. "It's got everything: hiking, skiing, hot air ballooning, water sports, nightclubs, and awesome weather. For concerts and cultural events places like Red Rocks Amphitheater, Fiddler's Green, and the Denver Center for the Performing Arts. Who could ask for more?"

Telluride attracts many of these young professionals. In late June there's the Bluegrass Festival, perhaps the finest in the country. For five full days and nights, amateur and professional bluegrass pickers perform and compete on banjos, mandolins, flat-picked guitars, and other instruments. The next month it's jazz, performed all weekend long in Town Park. In September, Telluride hosts a superb film festival.

Many young singles flock to Colorado ski areas each season to "ski bum"—work where they can ski. But finding affordable housing has become a big problem in recent years. The cost of living is so high in resort towns like Aspen, Vail, and Breckenridge

that service people can't afford to live there. "It was great when I worked at Eldora and lived in Boulder," says Todd, a twenty-year-old ski bum. "But when I tried it at Vail, there was no way I could make ends meet."

James Michener's *Centennial* paints a vivid picture of Colorado's people throughout time. The story begins before the dinosaurs and continues into the present. You meet Indian leaders Lame Beaver and Clay Basket; Pasquinale, a French *voyageur* who came to trap beaver, and his partner, Scotsman Alexander McKeag; pioneers who came west on covered wagons; ranchers and cowboys who rode the trails up from Texas. Michener's story is set in the fictional town of Centennial on the Platte River, near present day Kersey. His research was done in libraries and museums in Denver. Says Michener, "No city could have been more pleasant to work in than Denver, except for repeated traffic tickets, the worst winter in 170 years, [and] the hottest summer in 87 [years]."

"COLORADO: You Have To Ski It To Believe It"
                    —a popular bumper sticker

5 CELEBRATED COLORADANS

Christmas Walk in Denver's Larimer Square.

Songwriter John Denver, of *Rocky Mountain High* and *Aspenglow* fame, is one of many celebrities to adopt Aspen as home. The incredibly wealthy businessman Mohammed Hadid owns a palatial estate here. Radical journalist Hunter Thompson lives in nearby Woody Creek. Any afternoon you might see actor Jack Nicholson, television star Don Johnson, his ex-wife, actress Melanie Griffith, or other celebrities strolling the streets of town. In his book *White-out: Lost in Aspen*, Coloradan Ted Conover does a study of the town while working as a taxi driver and reporter for *The Aspen Times*. "In Aspen," Conover writes, "Peter Pan could find a Never-Never land."

ACTORS AND MUSICIANS

Colorado has put a number of famous faces on movie and television screens. Denver Pyle, born in Bethune in 1920, is best known for his roles in *Bonnie and Clyde, Life and Times of Grizzly Adams,* and the *Dukes of Hazzard*. Jan-Michael Vincent, born in Denver in 1944, had leading roles in *White Line Fever* and the television series *The Winds of War.*

A pioneer of movies in the days of the silent screen was Denverite Douglas Fairbanks. Abandoned by his father when he was five years old and resented by his mother because his skin was very dark,

Songwriter John Denver isn't really from Colorado and his name isn't really Denver. He's John Deutschendorf from Texas!

Douglas spent a mischievous childhood letting water snakes loose in Denver streetcars and putting vinegar into the wine to be served at church. In desperation, Douglas's mother sent him to Jarvis Military Academy, where he developed an interest in drama that would lead to fame. When he married Mary Pickford, an equally celebrated film star, they were considered the most popular couple the world had ever known. After his tremendous success in films such as *The Thief of Bagdad*, Fairbanks helped found the film company United Artists.

Folk singer Judy Collins, who rose to fame in the 1960s, also grew up in Denver. Her youngest brother was named Denver John because her father loved the city so much. "Daddy blossomed in Denver, with a new life, a new leaf," she recalled. At age thirteen, Collins performed a Mozart piano concerto with a symphony orchestra in Denver. But soon she abandoned classical music for

Denver-born Douglas Fairbanks, one of the first and greatest screen heroes of all time, was known as the "King of Hollywood" during the 1920s.

the guitar and turned to writing and performing such hit songs as *Both Sides Now* and *Send In the Clowns*.

ARTISTS AND WRITERS

Located in Old Colorado City near Colorado Springs and also at Writers' Square in Denver, is Michael Garman's Magic Town and Gallery. This world-famous Colorado Springs sculptor is known for his miniature dioramas of common scenes like barber shops or movie theaters. Many scenes feature holograms that add magic to the sculpture, like the one in a dentist's office. At first glance viewers see a dentist hovering over a patient in the chair. But look away for a split second, the office becomes dark, and the dentist is gone!

Popular Colorado Springs children's artist Michael Hague has illustrated such classic stories as *Hans Christian Andersen Fairy Tales* and *The Velveteen Rabbit*. In Hague's version of *The Wizard of Oz* he writes, "I count myself as one of the most fortunate of beings. For as an artist I have not only the pleasure but the duty to daydream. It is part of my work."

The state was also home to playwright and children's author

"Art for the people," is how sculptor Michael Garman describes his work. He wants his works to reach all kinds of people–rich, poor, young, and old.

WYNKEN, BLYNKEN & NOD

Eugene Field was a poet and writer who made his home in Denver in the late 1800s. He is best known for his characters Wynken, Blynken, and Nod, who have a statue in their honor in Denver's Washington Park. The poem begins:

> Wynken, Blynken, and Nod one night
> > Sailed off in a wooden shoe—
> Sailed on a river of crystal light,
> > Into a sea of dew.
>
> "Where are you going, and what do you wish?"
> The old moon asked the three.
> "We have come to fish for the herring fish
> That live in this beautiful sea;
> Nets of silver and gold have we!"
> > Said Wynken,
> > Blynken,
> > And Nod.

While they fished, they were entertained by the old moon and the stars, who laughed and sang songs to the voyagers:

> All night long their nets they threw
> > To the stars in the twinkling foam—
> Then down from the skies came the wooden shoe,
> > Bringing the fishermen home;
> 'Twas all so pretty a sail it seemed
> > As if it could not be,
> And some folks thought 'twas a dream they'd dreamed
> Of sailing that beautiful sea—
> But I shall name you the fisherman three:
> > Wynken,
> > Blynken,
> > And Nod.

Wynken and Blynken are two little eyes,
     And Nod is a little head,
And the wooden shoe that sailed the skies
     Is a wee one's trundle-bed.
So shut your eyes while mother sings
     Of wonderful sights that be,
And you shall see the beautiful things
     As you rock in the misty sea,
Where the old shoe rocked the fishermen three:
          Wynken,
          Blynken,
          And Nod.

Mary Coyle Chase, born in Denver in 1907. Chase is best known for the play *Harvey*, which received a Pulitzer Prize and ran on Broadway for nearly five years. Although the play was not written for children, the main character is a six-foot-tall white rabbit.

Modern day children's author Mary Calhoun lived in Steamboat Springs when she wrote her much-loved *Cross-Country Cat*. Henry, the Siamese feline hero, becomes a superb skier on boards fashioned by The Kid out of an old roof shingle. To practice his technique,

> Henry remembered a song The Kid used to sing, "This old man, he played one, he played knick-knack on my thumb . . . " Henry tried stepping his skis in time to the song. He sang, "Yow me-yowl, yow me-yowl, yow me-ow me-ow me-owl . . . " and his skis went step-and-slide, step-and-slide, over the snow in perfect rhythm.

Western writer Zane Grey was born in Ohio and trained as a dentist. But in the late 1800s he moved to the Rocky Mountain region and began writing. Some of his novels are set in Colorado, a state he loved and one where he spent a lot of time. In *The Mysterious Rider*, heroine Columbine is named after the state flower. *Raiders of Spanish Peaks* takes its name from two extinct volcanoes in southeastern Colorado. Through the eyes of a young girl who has just ridden in from Kansas, Grey expresses his love for the state: "Harriet stared. . . . Where and when could she ever have seen such a glorious spectacle? . . . This scene . . . was vivid, real, marvelous, elevating. Lonely and wild and grand—this Colorado!"

In the 1860s and 70s, when Helen Hunt Jackson lived and wrote, it was "unwomanly" for a female to be a published author, so she signed her works simply "H. H."

Author Helen Hunt Jackson's dying wish was to be buried within the sound of Seven Falls, outside Colorado Springs, the place she had adopted as her home. Jackson moved west about 1870 and took pity on the Indians for the way the U.S. government was treating them. She wrote two successful novels on the subject: *Century of Dishonor* and *Ramona*.

HEROES OF SCIENCE AND SPORTS

Weak and frail throughout his youth, environmentalist Enos Mills left his home in Kansas at age fourteen for the excitement of Colorado. He found it near Estes Park, where Longs Peak rises more than fourteen thousand feet. Upon reaching the summit after the first of two hundred and fifty ascents he would ultimately make upon the peak, Mills wrote, "What a roof garden is this pile of rusty rocks!" It was the beginning of a lifelong love affair with the region that climaxed in 1915, when part of his beloved Rocky Mountains became a national park.

In the science of electronics, Yugoslavian-born Nikola Tesla was known both as a madman and a genius. Tesla showed the world the basics of computers, missiles and robots long before any were invented. From his laboratory in Colorado Springs he created his own lightning flashes and lit lamps without wires from a distance of twenty miles. He is best known for the Tesla coil, which produces high voltages of high-frequency alternating electrical current and was used in the development of modern neon and fluorescent lights. It is said that when Tesla was experimenting with his coil, he caused the lights to dim throughout the city of Colorado Springs.

Colorado has produced five astronauts: Vance Brand, M. Scott Carpenter, L. Gordon Cooper, J. M. "Mike" Lounge, and John L. Swigert. In 1986, another Colorado name was added to space history when the *Challenger* space shuttle exploded, killing Ellison S. Onizuka and six other crew members. Onizuka was a graduate of the University of Colorado, where a *Challenger* Memorial has been erected in honor of the victims.

The state is also home to many sports figures. One of the biggest names in skiing, Wallace "Buddy" Werner of Steamboat Springs, was a member of the 1956, 1960, and 1964 Olympic ski teams. "Buddy rightly was considered . . . America's No. 1 alpine skier and one of the five or six best in the world," says Steamboat historian

John Rolfe Burroughs. After Buddy was killed in an avalanche in Switzerland in 1964, Storm Mountain outside Steamboat was renamed Mount Werner.

At the 1996 Summer Olympics in Atlanta, Georgia, Coloradan Amy Van Dyken became the first female American swimmer to win four gold medals. Although she was also an individual winner, Amy preferred working with team members in the relay competition. "That was so cool . . . it's what the whole Olympic thing is about. It was so fun to race *with* them instead of against them."

Amy Van Dyken express-es her joy at winning the gold in the fifty-meter freestyle—her fourth gold medal in the 1996 summer Olympics.

Colorado boxing champion William Harrison "Jack" Dempsey started fighting at age nineteen under the name "Kid Blackie."

Boxing is another sport to which Colorado has contributed world class champions. During the 1920s, World Heavyweight Boxer Jack Dempsey was almost a god to his adoring fans. Dempsey was nick-named the "Manassa Mauler" in honor of the Colorado town where he was born.

When he was a child, his father moved the family often. "One day we were in Manassa and the next day we were gone," Dempsey later wrote. From 1911 to 1916 he lived as a hobo in mining camps, begging for food and riding the rails in the dead of winter. This rough, wild life prepared him well for a career in boxing. He would hold onto the world title from 1919 to 1926.

TRANSPORTATION AND COMMUNICATIONS LEADERS

Otto Mears, who arrived in the United States as an orphan at age twelve, became the major road and railroad builder in southwest Colorado's rugged San Juan Mountains. His accomplishments earned him the nickname "Pathfinder of the San Juans."

Another pioneer in transportation was Freelan O. Stanley, who with his brother, Francis, invented the Stanley Steamer Car in 1896. F. O. is also famous as the builder of the Stanley Hotel in Estes Park, the setting for Stephen King's novel *The Shining*.

After the hotel opened in 1909, a fleet of Stanley Steamers transported guests up and down the steep, narrow canyon road to Estes Park. A quiet, elegant atmosphere prevailed in the hotel. No cowboy boots or hard-soled shoes were allowed. In the beautiful white-and-gold music room on the first floor was the grand piano that F. O. gave his wife on opening night. And in the hallways connecting the guestrooms were the sinister fire hoses that came to life in *The Shining*.

The Rocky Mountain News, one of Colorado's two major daily newspapers, was founded by William Newton Byers in 1859, the year of the gold rush. "We have done this," wrote Byers in the first issue, "because we wished to help mould [sic] and organize the new population, and because we thought it would pay." Apparently it did, for the paper is still published today.

Freelan O. Stanley, builder of the Stanley Hotel in Estes Park, worked with his brother Frank to invent this steam powered car, the Stanley Steamer, which broke the world speed record in 1906: one mile in 28.2 seconds, or 127 miles per hour!

The Denver Post gained fame when it was bought near the turn of the century by Frederick Gilmer Bonfils and Harry Heye Tammen. Bonfils and Tammen were a colorful pair who were very creative in their circulation wars with the News. They tried everything from a cross-country roller skating competition to a jackrabbit hunt on the eastern plains, to increase the Post's circulation. Vegetable munching rabbits created a big problem for farmers, and after the hunt "the grateful farmers muttered prayers for the Post and gathered the dead rabbits. " All one hundred thousand were taken to Denver and when "the wagons drew up in front of the Post . . . the band played, [and] the frozen hares were passed out to the poor by sixty patrolmen," recalled biographer, Gene Fowler.

ENTREPRENEURS

Fire Stix, the hot spicy cinnamon candies that helped make Jolly Rancher so successful, are a Colorado product. The Jolly Rancher Candy Company was started as a soft ice cream store in 1949 by Bill and Dorothy Harmsen. Today it is one of the largest candy companies in the United States.

Another Colorado company, known nationally for its herbal tea, is Celestial Seasonings, founded in 1972 by Mo Siegel and friends. Siegel's secret to making his company successful was finding just the right herbs in the Colorado mountains, drying them carefully, and putting them into handsewn tea bags. Celestial Seasonings, headquartered in Boulder, is a multimillion-dollar company today.

Also in Boulder is Leanin' Tree, the western greeting card publisher. People who like cards with a cowboy, Indian, or western flavor look for these cards with the logo of a tall, leaning evergreen tree. Visitors to Leanin' Tree can tour the gallery featuring the original artwork from the cards, set up by Ed Trumbell, the company's founder.

The nationally known luggage company Samsonite was started by Denver's Shwayder brothers in 1910. The Shwayders' first venture was manufacturing trunks. "Strong Enough To Stand On," read the motto, and the picture showed the five Shwayder brothers standing on one of their cases. Nearly a century later, Samsonite is one of the largest makers of trunks and suitcases in the world.

"History is people," writes Gladys Bueler in her book *Colorado's Colorful Characters*. "These sketches are molded from nuggets extracted from rich veins of historical information. . . . The mother lode is there in the libraries for those who wish to dig deeper."

6 THE GRAND CIRCLE TOUR

Ziegler Lake, above Snowmass Divide, near Aspen

Snowy mountain peaks, silvery mountain streams, peaceful shimmering lakes, incomparable camping grounds . . . all combine to place [Colorado] at the very front among tourist lands of the country. *—from Colorado For the Tourist*

Little has changed since this guidebook was written in 1912. Today, passengers flying into Denver International Airport are greeted by imitation snowy mountain peaks that form the roof of the terminal building. The nation's newest major airport covers a land area larger than San Francisco, Boston, and Miami combined! From the terminal, arriving passengers have a dramatic view of the Colorado Rockies and the skyline of downtown Denver. Let's begin our tour right here.

GOING DOWNTOWN

The birthplace of Denver is near the spot where Cherry Creek and the Platte River meet. Here, at Confluence Park, is the Forney Transportation Museum. If you like things with wheels, this is the place for you. Here is aviation heroine Amelia Earhart's roadster, the world's largest steam locomotive, a bicycle built for four, Prince Aly Khan's Rolls Royce Phantom I, and hundreds of other unique vehicles.

Many Coloradans were very upset that Denver International Airport opened more than a year late and cost $5.1 billion—more than twice the original estimate!

North of the park is KidSlope, run by the Denver Children's Museum, where you can learn to ski on plastic "snow" winter or summer. For kids who like to work with tools, the museum has a great woodworking shop. If science experiments are your thing, there's a lab filled with wires and batteries, chemicals, magnets, and other Mr. Wizard items. Budding movie directors will find a light room, sound room, and computer lab. There's truly something for everyone.

On a hill overlooking downtown Denver sits Colorado's gold-domed capitol, the gold donated by proud Colorado miners when the building was under construction. The fifteenth step of the long granite stairway leading to the entrance marks the spot that is exactly 5,280 feet, or one mile, above sea level. Later measurements proved that wrong, so a brass plaque was installed on the eighteenth step saying that this is truly the one-mile level. Inside the capitol, visitors can climb up into the gold dome. But signs warn those who are out of shape that there are ninety-three steps and it's harder to breathe in high altitude country!

Across Civic Park from the capitol is the United States Mint. Half of all coins in the United States are manufactured here—38 million coins a day, worth approximately $1.5 million. That's five billion coins a year! The Denver Mint holds the largest supply of gold in the United States outside Fort Knox, Kentucky.

Nearby is the Colorado History Museum, featuring exhibits on Native Americans, the gold rush, the Westward Movement, railroad building, and dozens of other interesting periods in Colorado's history. In the museum are trunks filled with period clothing and artifacts so kids can dress up like pioneer women, cowboys, miners, and others who peopled the early West.

THE BOULDER MOUNTAIN AREA

Boulder is home to the University of Colorado Buffalos, one of college football's finest teams. But football isn't the only athletic event in this city. The 10K Bolder Boulder attracts some thirty-five thousand running enthusiasts to Colorado each year on Memorial Day.

The sun shines more hours each year in Denver than in San Diego, California, or Miami Beach, Florida.

This is a liberal city, where almost anything goes—except smoking. Most Boulderites are very health and fitness conscious, and the city council recently voted a citywide ban on smoking.

Heading up Boulder Canyon, massive rock formations tower on both sides of the road, just a few feet from your car. Even if you strain your neck at the window, there are many places where you can't see the tops of the rocks. As you travel along the steep curves

PLACES TO SEE

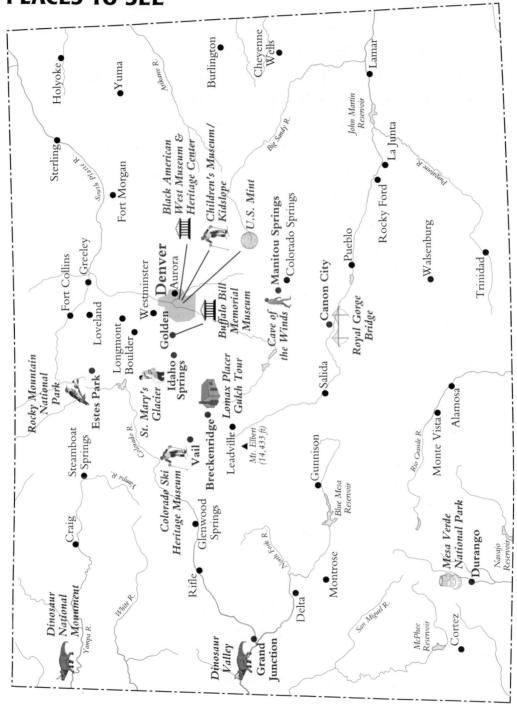

and narrow switchbacks of Colorado's canyon roads it becomes clear why these are called the Rocky Mountains.

Boulder Canyon takes travelers to the once quaint mining town of Central City, now a gambling center. On the floor of the Teller House (now a casino) is painted a picture of a mysterious woman named Madeline. Done by wandering artist Herndon Davis in 1936, this is "The Face on the Barroom Floor." The nearby Central City Opera House, still sporting some of the brass, wood, and red velvet decor from the late 1800s, holds excellent performances every summer.

The Peak to Peak Highway north from Central City leads to Estes Park, gateway to Rocky Mountain National Park. The scenery here is breathtaking, with more than one hundred peaks that reach ten thousand feet or higher. One of the nicest short hikes in the park is around Bear Lake where, on most days, you can see a spectacular reflection of Hallett Peak in the crystal blue water. Take a picnic, even in winter, as long as the sun is out to keep you warm! But watch out for gray jays, called camp robbers, who *will* sweep down and grab your sandwich.

If you're lucky you may spot a mountain goat, bear, moose, or mule deer. Spring and fall are better times to see elk and bighorn sheep, for when there's snow in the high country they move lower to find food. One of the most common of the 250 species of birds in the park is the Stellar's Jay, a gorgeous black-and-blue creature with a long crest on its head and white markings on its face.

Trail Ridge Road, the main route through the park, is the world's highest continuous paved highway. Snow, high winds, and poor visibility close the road from October to May, but during the sum-

Colorado's state animal, the sure-footed bighorn sheep, is found only in the Rocky Mountains.

mer travelers can cross the Continental Divide into the town of Grand Lake. Colorado's largest natural lake has the highest altitude yacht dock in America and is a popular sailing and fishing spot.

Along the way you'll see a parade of wild flowers—some nine hundred varieties grow in the park. Among them, you're sure to spot the blue columbine, Colorado's state flower, in groves of aspens—the trees that shimmer a gorgeous gold when their leaves turn in the fall.

COLORADO SPRINGS AND SOUTH

Another high altitude road trip is to the top of Pikes Peak, a trek made by thousands of tourists each year. The Pikes Peak Hill Climb

THE COLORADO TRAIL

To see Colorado by foot, the best route is along the Colorado Trail, a wilderness path running northeast/southwest across the state between Denver and Durango. The Colorado Trail (C.T.) is one of the most beautiful hikes in America, stretching 469 miles through Colorado's magnificent mountains. "The Colorado Trail," says *Backpacker* magazine editor Tom Shealey, "will take you places, both within and without."

Don't worry—you don't have to be an "end to end-er" to enjoy the C.T. There are many day hikes that are not rugged or grueling but offer the same spectacular scenery. If you do decide to tackle the entire trail, you'll pass through seven national forests, six wilderness areas, cross or parallel five major river systems, and pass through eight mountain ranges.

The building of the trail was undertaken by Gudy Gaskill, and before it was completed, more than three thousand teenage and adult volunteers had notched trees, moved or marked rocks, carved pathways, and moved dirt. Their help reduced the cost of building the trail from $8,000 a mile to only $500 a mile—and most volunteers admit they had a *wonderful* time doing it!

in mid-July is the second oldest auto race in America. Big-name drivers like Al Unser and Mario Andretti compete in the "Race to the Clouds." The Manitou & Pikes Peak Railway—highest railroad in the world—also carries sightseers to the top of the mountain.

The Colorado Springs area is filled with interesting spots. Young cowboys and cowgirls should visit the ProRodeo Hall of Fame and Museum of the American Cowboy. Here you can practice lassoing an iron bull's head, see exhibits of saddles, boots, cowboy hats, and other gear, and watch a variety of films about cowboys and rodeos.

The quaking aspen, so-called because of the almost constant trembling of its leaves, is the most widely distributed tree in North America.

Near Manitou Springs is Cave of the Winds, a real cave that has been filled with colored lights and paved pathways wide enough for a baby stroller. For visitors who have never been in a cave, it's a worthwhile trip. Those looking for a more realistic outdoor experience should visit the 1,350-acre Garden of the Gods park. Elephant Rock (you can actually see its trunk) and Balanced Rock (one on top of the other) are among the massive red sandstone formations. Near the park is the Manitou Cliff Dwellings Museum, a village of prehistoric Indian homes modeled after the Anasazi pueblos. The homes were built in 1907 with stones from original Indian dwellings. Since these are replicas, people are allowed to climb on and explore the "ruins."

South of the Springs, at Florissant Fossil Beds National Monument, volcanic ash has preserved a 35- to 40-million-year-old rain forest. The Petrified Forest Loop, a mile-long hiking trail, takes visitors to Big Stump, the remains of an ancient giant sequoia tree. South of Florissant is Cripple Creek, once called "the World's Greatest Gold Camp" and today a gambling center. To relive the mining days, tour the one-thousand-foot-deep Mollie Kathleen Mine, which operated until the early 1960s.

Spectacular Royal Gorge, near Canon City west of Pueblo, was carved nearly three million years ago by the Arkansas River. Rock walls rise 1,053 feet up the side of this awesome canyon. Winding along the bottom on the narrow bank is the track of the Southern Pacific Railway. Spanning the top of the gorge is the world's highest suspension bridge, built in 1929. The world's steepest incline railway takes visitors to the bottom of "Royal Gorgeous" in an elevator-like cage.

SEEING COLORADO BY TRAIN

Amtrak's California Zephyr runs east/west across the state. The ride from Denver west to Grand Junction offers more than two hundred miles of the grandest scenery anywhere in the United States. Soon after leaving Denver the train begins a slow, steep climb to the Continental Divide, passing through twenty-eight tunnels that burrow through huge spires of rock.

After emerging at Winter Park Ski Area on the west side of the 6.2-mile-long Moffat Tunnel, the train heads across broad, flat North Park, where ranching is a major business. Near Granby, the track joins the Colorado River, and the two run somewhat parallel throughout the rest of the trip.

The first of the river's spectacular canyons is just east of Glenwood Springs. This spa and resort town is home to the world's largest outdoor mineral hot springs pool. The swimming pool, as long as two city blocks, averages 90 degrees F. The smaller therapy pool is kept at 104 degrees. Glenwood Springs is the home of the teddy bear. President Theodore (Teddy) Roosevelt, who loved to hunt, stayed at the elegant Hotel Colorado while visiting the Rockies. After one unsuccessful expedition, a chambermaid felt sorry for him and made a stuffed bear that his daughter named "Teddy's bear."

West of Glenwood, passengers head through beautiful Byers Canyon near Hot Sulphur Springs. The town was named for the rich mineral springs located there. Farther west is gorgeous Gore Canyon with its picture-book spires of rock rising steeply on either side of the river. Beyond that, heading into the plateau region, the train passes through oil shale and book cliff country. The Book

Cliffs are sandstone formations shaped exactly like their name. To the south, in the distance, is Grand Mesa, the world's largest flat-top mountain.

Ahead lies Grand Junction, named because it is the meeting point of the Colorado (formerly the Grand River) and the Gunnison. Just west of the city is Colorado National Monument, a fairyland of deep canyons and natural rock sculptures with names like "Praying Hands" and "Kissing Couple." Wrote explorer John Otto in the early 1900s, "I came here last year and found these canyons, and they felt like the heart of the world to me."

SOUTHWEST BY CAR

From Grand Junction, our Grand Circle Tour heads south by car along the beautiful Dolores River, to the southwestern corner of the state. Here is Mesa Verde National Park where the ancient Anasazi ruins and cliff dwellings are preserved. From nearby Durango, travelers can ride on an 1880s narrow gauge steam train. The Durango & Silverton carries passengers round-trip through the mountains to the quaint old mining town of Silverton.

Our return to the east passes near Great Sand Dunes National Monument. These dunes are mountains of sand that rise to peaks about seven hundred feet high and cover a strip thirty-nine miles long. They were formed when eroding rock and sediment, tossed by the constant southwest winds, settled at the base of the Sangre de Cristo (Blood of Christ) mountains. Children love to ride sheets of cardboard down these sand mountains or "ski" downhill on their bare feet.

Men To Match My
Mountains
—*title of a book about
the American West by
Irving Stone*

The road north from the Sand Dunes goes into Colorado's highest mountains. Among the giants are the Collegiate Peaks: Yale,
Princeton, Harvard, Columbia, and Oxford—all of them towering
above fourteen thousand feet—and the state's highest, Mount
Elbert. The nearby city of Buena Vista on the Arkansas River claims
to be the whitewater rafting capital of the world.

Farther north is Fairplay, just eighteen miles from the geo-
graphic center of Colorado, and the center of the South Park gold

rush in 1859. Today a living replica of South Park City (Fairplay's original name) includes stores, offices, saloons, a school, and homes just as they were in the gold rush days.

From Fairplay our tour heads back to Denver through Golden. At the Colorado School of Mines is the National Earthquake Information Center. When an earthquake erupts anywhere in the world, the center transmits information by computer to scientists and agencies worldwide. If you like trains, stop at the Colorado Railroad Museum where more than fifty locomotives, railway cars, and other railroad items are on display.

For a hair-raising ride, a beautiful view, an interesting museum, and a close-up look at hang gliders, drive up Lookout Mountain near Golden. More than a half million people make the trip each year to catch this breathtaking view of the Great Plains. At the top is Buffalo Bill's grave and the Pa-Ha-Ska Tepee museum with all sorts of objects from his Wild West performances.

The return to Denver completes our Grand Circle tour of Colorado. But for every stop, there are dozens that were not made. We could have visited the Mountain Bike Hall of Fame in Crested Butte or ridden the Platte Valley Trolley in Denver. We might have viewed the Living Trees in Sterling where sculptors have carved trunks to look like giraffes and other objects. On a February tour we could have stopped in Loveland to get our Valentines stamped with a special postmark from "Love Land." But don't despair. Your stamped Valentines will be canceled for you if you send them in an envelope to the main post office. For all the other great sights and more, however, you'll have to make another trip to the Centennial State.

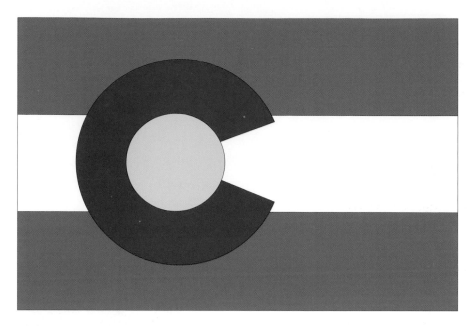

THE FLAG: The state flag has three equal bands running horizontally. The top and bottom bands are blue and the middle band is white. A large red "C" for Colorado surrounds a golden disk. The flag was adopted in 1911.

THE SEAL: The state seal has a shield whose top part has three snow-capped mountains with clouds above. The bottom part shows a miner's pick and mallet. Above the shield is the eye of God inside a pyramid and a Roman fasces, a bundle of sticks with an ax at the center. The fasces represents our republican form of government. Below the shield is the state motto in Latin. The words "State of Colorado 1876" frame the picture. The seal was adopted in 1877.

STATE SURVEY

Statehood: August 1, 1876

Origin of Name: Colorado takes its name from the Colorado River. The river was named for the red canyons through which it flows. *Colorado* is a Spanish word meaning "color red."

Nickname: Centennial State

Capital: Denver

Motto: Nothing Without Providence

Bird: Lark bunting

Animal: Rocky Mountain bighorn sheep

Flower: Rocky Mountain columbine

Tree: Colorado blue spruce

Gem: Aquamarine

Fossil: Stegosaurus

Rocky Mountain columbine

Lark bunting

GEOGRAPHY

Highest Point: 14,433 feet above sea level at Mount Elbert

WHERE THE COLUMBINES GROW

The white and lavender Rocky Mountain columbine was declared the state flower April 4, 1899. In 1915, after a camping trip, Professor Arthur J. Flynn of Denver wrote this tribute to the beautiful flower. The graceful waltz was adopted as the state song that same year.

Lowest Point: 3,350 feet above sea level along the Arkansas River in Prowers County

Area: 104,091 square miles

Greatest Distance, North to South: 276 miles

Greatest Distance, East to West: 387 miles

Bordering States: Wyoming and Nebraska to the north, Oklahoma and New Mexico to the south, Nebraska and Kansas to the east, and Utah to the west

Hottest Recorded Temperature: 118° F at Bennett on July 11, 1888

Coldest Recorded Temperature: -61° F at Maybell on February 1, 1985

Average Annual Precipitation: 15 inches

Major Rivers: Animas, Arkansas, Blue, Colorado, Dolores, Gunnison, North Platte, Republican, Rio Grande, San Juan, South Platte, White, Yampa

Major Lakes: Blue Mesa, Dillon, Granby, Grand, McPhee, Meredith, Pueblo, Shadow Mountain, Summit

Trees: ash, aspen, blue spruce, cottonwood, Douglas fir, Engelmann spruce, juniper, maple, oak, piñon pine, ponderosa pine

Wild Plants: buttercup, cactus, columbine, daisy, forget-me-not, greasewood, Indian paintbrush, larkspur, mountain lily, pasqueflower, prickly poppy, orchid, sagebrush, violet, wild geranium, wild iris, wild rose, yucca

Animals: antelope, beaver, black bear, bobcat, coyote, elk, fox, jackrabbit,

Rocky Mountain bighorn sheep

marmot, marten, mountain goat, mountain lion, mule deer, pika, prairie dog, Rocky Mountain bighorn sheep, skunk

Birds: bald eagle, bluebird, blue jay, brown thrasher, duck, grouse, hermit thrush, lark bunting, meadowlark, mountain chickadee, mourning dove, oriole, peregrine falcon, pheasant, prairie chicken, quail, Rocky Mountain jay

Fish: bass, bluegill, catfish, crappie, perch, salmon, sunfish, trout

Endangered Animals: bald eagle, bonytail, gray wolf, greater prairie chicken, greater sandhill crane, greenback cutthroat trout, grizzly bear, humpback chub, lynx, peregrine falcon, piping plover, razorback sucker, river otter, Uncompahgre fritillary butterfly, whooping crane, wolverine, wood frog

Endangered Plants: clay-loving wild-buckwheat, Dudley Bluffs bladderpod, Dudley Bluffs twinpod, Manco's milk-vetch, North Park phacelia, Osterhout milk-vetch, Penland beardtongue, spineless hedgehog cactus, Uinta Basin hookless cactus

TIMELINE

Colorado History

c. A. D. 1 The Basketmakers settle in the Mesa Verde region

c. 750 The people at Mesa Verde begin building pueblos, or large, apartment-like dwellings, in the sides of cliffs

c. 1300 The Pueblo people of Mesa Verde mysteriously abandon their cliff dwellings

1598 Juan de Oñate is the first European to reach the area of present-day Colorado

1706 Juan de Ulibarri claims the Arkansas River Valley for Spain

1765 Juan Maria de Rivera explores the area of the San Juan Mountains and the Gunnison River

1803 The United States receives much of northeastern Colorado through the Louisiana Purchase

1806 Zebulon Pike explores Colorado and sees the mountain that will bear his name

1848 The United States receives western Colorado from Mexico after America's victory in the Mexican-American War

1851 The first permanent non-Native American settlement in Colorado is established at San Luis

1858 Gold is discovered near Pikes Peak; thousands of miners rush to Colorado in the Pikes Peak Gold Rush

1859 Gold is discovered along Clear Creek and at other sites in Colorado

1860 Auraria and Denver City merge to form Denver

1861 The Colorado Territory is formed

1861–1865 The Civil War

1864 Cheyennes and Arapahos are massacred by Colorado militia at Sand Creek

1867 Denver is named territorial capital

1868 American soldiers survive a nine-day siege by Cheyenne and Sioux at Beecher Island

1869 The last battle between U.S. soldiers and Native Americans is fought at Summit Springs on the Colorado plains

1870 The Denver Pacific and Kansas Pacific railroads connect Colorado to the eastern United States

1876 Colorado becomes the thirty-eighth state

1877 A silver strike at Leadville leads to a silver boom for Colorado

1890 Gold is discovered at Cripple Creek

1894 Women are allowed to vote in Colorado elections for the first time

1906 The United States Mint in Denver begins producing coins

1914 A coal miners' strike in southern Colorado leads to the shooting deaths of several people by the National Guard in the Ludlow Massacre

1917–1918 43,000 Coloradans serve in the armed forces in World War I

1929 The bridge across the Royal Gorge, the world's highest suspension bridge at the time, opens

1930s Drought and winds turn Colorado's plains into a "Dust Bowl," bringing disaster to farmers during the Great Depression

1942 Ten thousand Japanese Americans are brought to internment camps near Grenada because of fears they might aid Japan during World War II

1958 The United States Air Force Academy opens near Colorado Springs

1959 The Colorado-Big Thompson Project for supplying irrigation to Colorado farmland is completed

1966 The headquarters of the North American Air Defense Command are completed deep within Cheyenne Mountain

1976 Flooding along the Big Thompson kills over 100 people

1983 Federico Peña becomes the first Hispanic mayor of Denver

1995 Denver's $5.1 billion, state-of-the-art airport opens

ECONOMY

Agricultural Products: apples, barley, beans, cattle, cherries, chickens, corn, dairy products, eggs, hay, hogs, onions, peaches, potatoes, sheep and lambs, sorghum, sugar beets, wheat

Manufactured Products: computers, electrical equipment, fabricated metal products, medical instruments, mining machinery, office equipment, printed materials, scientific instruments, soft drinks and beer

Natural Resources: coal, copper, gold, granite, lead, limestone, molybdenum, natural gas, petroleum, sand and gravel, silver, tungsten, uranium, vanadium, zinc

Business and Trade: communications, data processing, engineering, finance, insurance, real estate, tourism, transportation, wholesale and retail sales

CALENDAR OF CELEBRATIONS

National Western Stock Show and Rodeo Every January Denver hosts the world's biggest livestock show. The celebration starts with a parade, followed by a rodeo, livestock auctions, and a petting arena for children.

Winter Carnival The longest-running winter fair west of the Mississippi River is held in Steamboat Springs every February. The carnival includes a week's worth of downhill and cross-country ski races, ski-jumping, and other winter fun.

Denver Powwow Native Americans from almost seventy cultures gather for this annual March event. Visitors can watch Native American dancers, drummers, and artists celebrate their traditional ways.

Crane Festival This March festival celebrates the spring return of whooping and sandhill cranes to the San Luis Valley. There are bus tours, art exhibits, and lectures on wildlife during this Monte Vista festival.

Mountain Man Rendezvous Visitors to this annual April event can view a reenactment of Colorado's mountain man days with period costumes, axe-throwing and black powder shooting contests, and period cooking and crafts. This colorful festival is held in Kit Carson.

Territory Days Every May, Colorado's pre-state history is celebrated in Colorado Springs. Events include games, contests, and a make-believe gunfight.

Cinco de Mayo This traditional Mexican holiday honoring a Mexican military victory over French forces in 1862 is celebrated in Denver every May 5. The festival features ethnic foods, music, and dancing.

Aspen Music Festival Artists known around the world come to Aspen to perform classical and chamber music, as well as opera at this nine-week festival that begins in June. Bring a picnic and sit on the lawn around several concert sites to hear some beautiful music.

Strawberry Days This Glenwood Springs festival features a carnival, arts and crafts, and lots of strawberries. The celebration is held every June.

Bluegrass Festival Bluegrass and country music are the main attractions at this June festival. You can listen to the great sounds outdoors in Telluride.

Aerial Weekend Look to the skies for this July festival in Crested Butte. There are hot-air balloons, hang gliding, and fun activities for kids.

Dinosaur Days Visitors to this festival can watch a dinosaur parade, participate in a fossil dig, and listen to band concerts. Dinosaur Days are held in July in Grand Junction.

Pikes Peak Highland Games and Celtic Festival The region's Scottish heritage is celebrated during this July festival held in Colorado Springs. Traditional Scottish games are played, and there is music, dancing, and food.

Folklife Festival This July festival celebrates folk traditions and arts and crafts from Colorado's

Pikes Peak Highland Games and Celtic Festival

European, Native American, and Hispanic past. The celebration happens in Buena Vista.

Boom Days Leadville hosts this August festival in memory of the gold and silver booms of long ago. Mine drilling competitions and a pack burro race are the highlights of the festival, but there's also a carnival, music, and food.

Colorado State Fair All of the best of Colorado can be enjoyed at the state fair. There are livestock shows and auctions, rides, food, and big-time entertainment. The fair starts in August in Pueblo.

Vail Fest Street entertainment, a yodeling contest, and foot races are just a part of this Vail celebration. The September festival also has sing-alongs, games, and dancing.

Apple Fest This annual October event in Cedaredge celebrates the region's apple harvest. The festival includes arts and crafts, square dancing, and food.

Western Arts, Film, and Cowboy Poetry Gathering Real cowboys gather in Durango in October to share their poetry. The celebration also features demonstrations of cowboy skills, art, and film.

Catch the Glow Estes Park celebrates the holiday season with this November event. The celebration includes holiday lights, clowns, puppeteers, carolers, and an evening parade.

Christmas 1846 at Bent's Old Fort See what Christmas was like on the old frontier. This reenactment brings holidays past to life in this December celebration in La Junta.

STATE STARS

Katharine Lee Bates (1859–1929) was a college professor from the East. The view from the top of Pikes Peak in 1893 inspired her to write the words to "America the Beautiful."

Jim Beckwourth (1798–1867?), an African-American mountain man, ran trading posts in the Rocky Mountains. He is also believed to have founded and named the town of Pueblo.

William Bent (1809–1869) was a prominent trader in Colorado in the early part of the nineteenth century. Along with his brothers, Bent built Bent's Fort in 1833–1834.

Albert Bierstadt (1830–1902) painted beautiful scenes of Colorado, such as *Storm in the Rocky Mountains.* His works helped bring attention to Colorado's natural setting.

Black Kettle (?–1868) was a Cheyenne leader whose village was destroyed in the 1864 Sand Creek Massacre, even though he had agreed to peace with the U.S. government. Black Kettle was later killed by U.S. troops when his village in what is today Oklahoma was attacked.

Clara Brown

Clara Brown (1803–1885), a former slave, moved to Colorado during the 1859 gold rush. Her home in Central City became a boardinghouse for poor miners as well as a hospital and church.

Margaret Tobin (Molly) Brown (1873–1932), originally of Missouri, became wealthy through the Colorado silver industry. Brown survived the wreck of the "unsinkable" Titanic, helping a lifeboat full of passengers stay alive, and earned her nickname "the Unsinkable Molly Brown."

Ben Nighthorse Campbell (1933–   ) is a U.S. senator from Colorado. Campbell, a Native American, is known for dressing in Cheyenne costume on special occasions and for his support of Native American issues.

Scott Carpenter (1925–   ) was born in Boulder. As one of the United States' early astronauts, Carpenter was the second American to orbit Earth during the Mercury 4 mission.

Scott Carpenter

Lon Chaney

Kit Carson (1809–1868) earned fame as a trapper and scout in Colorado and the West. He also ran a trading post at what is now the town bearing his name.

Lon Chaney (1883–1930) was an early big screen actor best known for his roles in horror films, such as *The Hunchback of Notre Dame* and *The Phantom of the Opera*. Born in Colorado Springs, Chaney was known as the "man of a thousand faces."

Mary Chase (1907–1981) won the 1945 Pulitzer Prize for her play *Harvey*, about a man whose best friend is an imaginary, six-foot-tall rabbit. Chase was born in Denver.

Chipeta (1843–1924) was the wife of the Ute leader Ouray. Like her husband, Chipeta worked to maintain the peace between Native Americans and settlers in Colorado.

Adolph Coors (1847–1919) came to Golden from his native Germany. In Golden, he founded the Adolph Coors Company in 1880. The company has since grown to become one of the country's largest beer makers.

Jack Dempsey (1895–1983) was the world heavyweight boxing champion from 1919 to 1926. Born in Manassa, he became known as the "Manassa Mauler."

John Denver (1943–1997) is a singer/songwriter originally from Texas. Born Henry John Deutschendorf, he changed his name because of his love for the city. His songs have included "Rocky Mountain High" and "I Guess I'd Rather Be in Colorado." Denver has also acted, and his film credits include *Oh, God*. He lives in Aspen.

Ralph Edwards (1913–   ), from Merino, has produced a number of well-known television shows. Some of the shows Edwards has worked on include *Truth or Consequences*, *This Is Your Life*, *Name that Tune*, and *The People's Court*.

John Elway (1960–   ) has been an outstanding quarterback for the Denver Broncos. His exciting style of play has led the Broncos to three Super Bowls—in 1987, 1988, and 1990.

John Elway

John Evans (1814–1897) was the territorial governor of Colorado from 1862 to 1865. He founded the school that was to become the University of Denver, and in 1870 he built the Denver Pacific Railroad, which linked Colorado to the rest of the country.

Douglas Fairbanks (1883–1939), born in Denver, starred in many action movies in the early years of film. His credits include *The Three Musketeers* and *Robin Hood*. He also helped found the United Artists film company.

Barney Ford (1824–1902) was a fugitive from slavery who joined the Colorado gold rush in 1860. He became the owner of a well-known Denver hotel and helped other fugitive slaves. Ford also started the first classes for African-American adults in Colorado.

Justina Ford (1871–1952) was the first African-American woman to become a doctor in Colorado. Ford delivered thousands of babies, mainly for poor black women, in Denver.

Willard Libby (1908–1980) of Grand Valley achieved fame as a chemist by discovering a way to determine the age of prehistoric materials using radiocarbon testing. He won the 1960 Nobel Prize in chemistry.

Glenn Miller (1904–1944) grew up in Fort Morgan and attended the University of Colorado. Miller gained fame as a trombone player and leader of the Glenn Miller Band. He died on his way to entertain American troops in World War II when the plane he was flying in was lost.

Ouray (1820–1880) was a Ute leader who attempted to keep the peace between Native Americans and settlers. His efforts helped to maintain good relations between the two groups for many years.

David Packard (1912–   ) grew up in Pueblo. In 1939, Packard started the Hewlett-Packard Company along with William Hewlett. The company became an electronics giant and today makes computers.

Frederico Peña

Federico Peña (1947–   ), a Mexican American, served two terms as mayor of Denver, from 1983 to 1991. Peña was later picked by President Bill Clinton to lead the U.S. Department of Transportation.

Antoinette Perry (1888–1946), born in Denver, was a popular stage actress in the early 1900s. The Tony Award, which is given each year to the best actors in theater, is named for Perry, whose nickname was Tony.

Zebulon Pike (1779–1813) was a famous explorer of the American West. Pike first spotted the mountain which was named after him in 1806.

Denver Pyle (1920–   ), from Bethune, is a well-known face in the movies and on television. Pyle has had roles in *Bonnie and Clyde*, *The Life and Times of Grizzly Adams*, and *The Dukes of Hazzard*.

Florence Sabin (1871–1953) became well known for her medical work with the disease tuberculosis. She was the first woman chosen to join the National Academy of Sciences. Sabin was born in Central City.

Florence Sabin

Patricia Schroeder

Patricia Schroeder (1940–   ) was Colorado's first female to serve in the U.S. Congress. Schroeder was first elected to the House of Representatives in 1973.

Byron White (1917–   ) was born in Fort Collins. A college and pro football star, White studied law and was named to the U.S. Supreme Court by President John F. Kennedy in 1962.

TOUR THE STATE

Dinosaur National Monument (Dinosaur) While the dinosaur bones are found in the Utah side of this national site, the Colorado side offers beautiful views and hiking trails.

Hot Springs Pool (Glenwood Springs) Heated by mineral hot springs to a temperature of 90° F, the pool here is over two blocks long and open year round. There's also a huge, twisting water slide.

Colorado Ski Heritage Museum (Vail) The history of skiing in Colorado is presented through pictures and artifacts, such as old skis and chairlifts, at this museum. There is also a video on the history of Vail.

Lomax Placer Gulch Tour (Breckenridge) Tour a miner's cabin and find out how Colorado's old-time miners searched for gold at this fun site. You can even swirl a miner's pan in water to find some flecks of real gold.

Rocky Mountain National Park (Estes Park) This beautiful national park offers everything from fishing to hiking to rock climbing. The park has some 355 miles of hiking trails, many of which are suitable for children.

Georgetown Viewing Station (Georgetown) Through the viewing scopes at this station you can often spot Rocky Mountain bighorn sheep during the winter. You may even be able to hear the crack of the male sheep's horns as they fight for leadership of the herd.

St. Mary's Glacier (Idaho Springs) Not only can you view a glacier here, you can actually walk on it. Scenic hiking paths travel around St. Mary's Lake and up to the glacier.

Buffalo Bill Memorial Museum and Grave (Golden) One of the West's greatest legends, Buffalo Bill Cody, is remembered in this museum. Learn about his life through the dioramas, artifacts, clothes, photos, and paintings on display here.

Black American West Museum and Heritage Center (Denver) Learn about the history of African Americans in the American West, especially African-American cowboys, through the artifacts and pictures in this museum located in a historic Denver home.

Children's Museum (Denver) Reporting the weather on the museum's TV station, exploring a beehive, or touching a live snake are just a few of the things you can do here. Outside the museum is Kidslope, an artificial ski slope where visitors can learn to ski year-round.

Denver Museum of Natural History (Denver) You can learn about everything from dinosaurs to gold nuggets to the stars at this exciting museum. At the Hall of Life, visitors can test and learn about their own fitness.

U.S. Mint (Denver) A tour of Denver's mint reveals how the coins jingling in your pocket are made. Visitors can see new coins pouring out of stamping machines and being counted and bagged.

Plains Conservation Center (Aurora) Animals inside the center include badgers, prairie dogs, coyotes, jackrabbits, owls, and eagles. Special guided tours offer chances to see the wildlife and plants of the prairie and hear educational lectures.

Historic Centennial Village (Greeley) The buildings at this site reflect life in Colorado from 1860 to 1920. There are several homes, ranging from a mansion to a homestead shack; a schoolhouse, a teepee, a blacksmith shop, and more.

Cave of the Winds (Manitou Springs) Narrow passages and winding paths take you through 20 underground rooms, full of impressive stalagmites and stalactites. There is also an outdoor laser light show held in the evenings.

Garden of the Gods (Colorado Springs) Incredible red sandstone formations are the attraction at this impressive site. Stone formations with names like Balanced Rock and Kissing Camels glow brightly in the rising or setting sun.

Kissing Camels Rock, Garden of the Gods

United States Air Force Academy (Colorado Springs) Visitors to the Academy can see a short film about the school, and watch as cadets march to the dining hall and practice parachute jumps. The Cadet Chapel is one of Colorado's most recognized buildings.

Pikes Peak and Pike National Forest (Colorado Springs) Beautiful views are the prime attraction of a climb up Pikes Peak. Denver, 75 miles away, can often be seen from the top. The summit can be reached by trail, road, or cog railway.

El Pueblo Museum (Pueblo) The exhibits at this museum explore the heritage of the Pueblo area. There are saddles on which to climb, a full-size teepee to explore, and displays on children's clothing from the nineteenth century.

Bent's Old Fort National Historic Site (La Junta) The fort here is a reconstruction of Bent's Fort as it looked in 1845. Visitors can explore such areas as the kitchen, blacksmith and carpenter shops, and rooms that would have been the quarters of trappers and soldiers.

Royal Gorge Bridge (Canon City) The Royal Gorge Bridge is the highest suspension bridge in the world and a walk across it can be exciting and scary. There is also an aerial tram that goes over the gorge and an incline railway with tracks going up the side of the gorge to ride.

Great Sand Dunes National Monument (Alamosa) The dunes at this site can reach 700 feet high, the tallest in North America. Hiking over the dunes is permitted, though it can be tiring work.

Mesa Verde National Park (Durango) Exploring this amazing site, the home of the region's Anasazi people 700 years ago, often requires climbing

10-foot ladders and crawling through tunnels. A museum here helps explain the Anasazi culture and their cliff-side homes.

Black Canyon of the Gunnison (Montrose) The 2,500-foot-high walls of this canyon make for breathtaking views. In some places, the walls seem to have been painted by an artist. The area has many short hiking trails.

Fort Uncompahgre Living History Museum (Delta) Dressed as the inhabitants of the fort would have been in 1826, guides help bring this site alive. They carry out everyday activities at this re-created fur trading post and allow visitors to join in.

Dinosaur Valley (Grand Junction) This attraction has giant robotic dinosaurs as well as real dinosaur skeletons and footprints. You can even watch workers at the lab as they carefully chip away at rock to reveal fossils.

FUN FACTS

The only city in the United States that gets its water from the melting ice of a glacier is Boulder. Boulder's water supply comes from the Arapahoe Glacier, northwest of the city.

In 1929, Bill Williams rolled a peanut to the top of Pikes Peak using his nose. The task took him 20 days.

A 1990 hailstorm, the most costly in United States history, caused $650-million-worth of damage in Colorado.

The two largest dinosaur skeletons ever discovered are from Colorado. Both were found in the 1970s south of Grand Junction.

The Barbie doll was invented by a Denver woman named Ruth Handler in 1959.

FIND OUT MORE

To find out more about the Mile-High State, check your school or local library or a good bookstore for these items. The first series was edited and published especially for Colorado school children by the author of this book, Eleanor Ayer.

GENERAL STATE BOOKS

Ayer, Eleanor H., editor. *The Colorado Chronicles, Vols. 1–8.* Frederick, CO: Platte 'N Press:

> Volume 1, *Famous Colorado Men,* 1980.
> Volume 2, *Famous Colorado Women,* 1981.
> Volume 3, *Indians of Colorado,* 1981.
> Volume 4, *Hispanic Colorado,* 1982.
> Volume 5, *Colorado Wildlife,* 1983.
> Volume 6, *Colorado Businesses,* 1984.
> Volume 7, *Colorado Wonders,* 1986.
> Volume 8, *Chronicles Index,* 1986.

———. *Colorado Traveler Hall of Fame.* Frederick, CO: Renaissance House Publishers, 1987.

Carpenter, Allan. *Enchantment of America: Colorado.* Chicago: Childrens Press, 1978.

Clarke, Phyllis J.; Downey, Matthew T.; Metcalf, Fay D. Colorado: *Crossroads of the West.* Boulder, CO: Pruett Publishing Co., 1977.

Hafen, LeRoy R. & Hafen, Ann. *Our State: Colorado*. Boulder, CO: Old West Textbooks, 1977.

Meitus, Marty & Thorn, Patti. *Places to Go With Children in Colorado*. San Francisco: Chronicle Books, 1995.

Midwest Research Institute & Capper Press. *The Colorado Quick-Fact Book*. Topeka, KS: Capper Press, 1992.

VIDEOS

American Automobile Association. *Colorado*. International Video Corporation, 1991.

Finley, Bill. *Explore Colorado*. Finley Holiday Film Corporation, 1987.

————. *Discover Pike's Peak Country Colorado*. Finley Holiday Film Corporation, no date.

McGuire, Leo with Bob Palmer. *Colorado Getaways*. Denver: Colorado Tourism Board, 1986.

Michener, James A. *Centennial*. Universal City, CA: MCA Universal Home Video, 1995.

WEBPAGE

http://www.state.co.us/colorado.htm/

This is Colorado's frequently updated homepage.

INDEX

Page numbers for illustrations are in boldface.